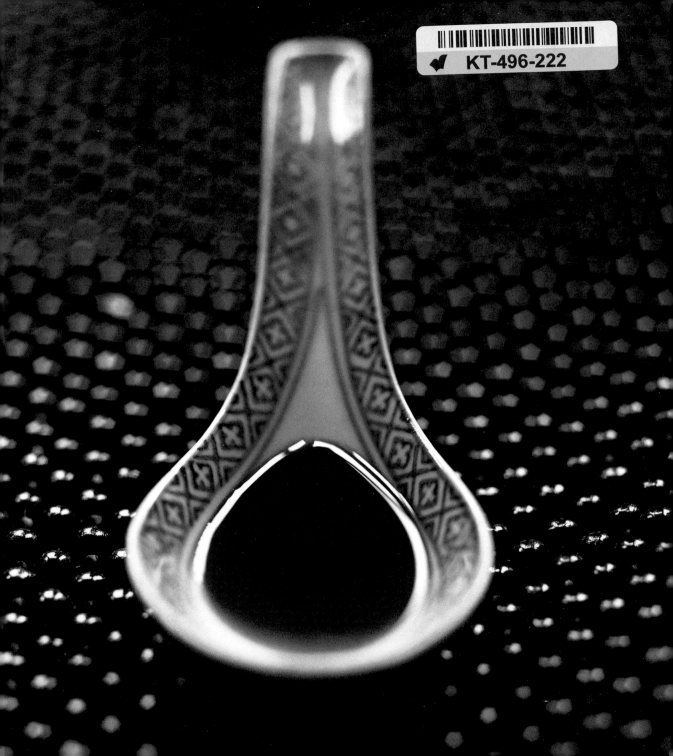

FRESH CHINESE

WYNNIE CHAN

hamlyn

TO LI LI AND TIMMY, FOR THEIR ENTHUSIASM ABOUT NEW FOODS.

First published in Great Britain in 2007 by
Hamlyn, a division of Octopus Publishing Group Ltd
2–4 Heron Quays, London E14 4JP

The material in this book was previously published in
Fresh Chinese

SBN-13: 978-0-600-61684-9
ISBN-10: 0-600-61684-3

A CIP catalogue record for this book is available from the
British Library

Printed and bound in China

10 9 8 7 6 5 4 3 2 1

NOTE

Both metric and imperial measurements have been given
in all recipes. Use one set of measurements only, and not a
mixture of both.

Standard level spoon measurements are used in all recipes.
1 tablespoon = one 15 ml spoon
1 teaspoon = one 5 ml spoon

The Department of Health advises that eggs should not be
consumed raw. This book contains dishes made with raw or
lightly cooked eggs. It is prudent for vulnerable people such as
pregnant and nursing mothers, invalids, the elderly, babies and
young children to avoid uncooked or lightly cooked dishes
made with eggs. Once prepared, these dishes should be kept
refrigerated and used promptly.

This book includes dishes made with nuts and nut derivatives. It is
advisable for customers with known allergic reactions to nuts and
nut derivatives and those who may be potentially vulnerable to
these allergies, such as pregnant and nursing mothers, invalids,
the elderly, babies and children to avoid dishes made with nuts
and nut oils. It is also prudent to check the labels of pre-prepared
ingredients for the possible inclusion of nut derivatives.

Ovens should be pre-heated to the specified temperature – if
using a fan-assisted oven, follow the manufacturer's instruc-
tions for adjusting the time and the temperature.

CONTENTS

FOREWORD BY KEN HOM

Cardiovascular ailments, such as heart disease and strokes, are the main cause of death in the UK and according to figures from the British Heart Foundation they account for more than 235,000 victims every year. One reason for such a high rate is that our diets are high in saturated fat but comparatively low in fresh fruit and vegetables.

Traditionally, the Chinese diet is low in fat and high in fruit and vegetables, so the fact that its popularity among the UK population has grown enormously over the past 50 years should be beneficial. According to a study published by the Institute of Grocery Distribution in 2002, Chinese food (including takeaways, ready meals and restaurant meals) was the most popular ethnic cuisine in the UK and was preferred by 58 per cent of consumers. However, bad Chinese takeaway food is greasy and unhealthy and is also high in salt and monosodium glutamate (MSG), factors that may increase our risk of cardiovascular problems.

Recognizing the need to encourage the adoption of a healthier diet, the British Heart Foundation in collaboration with the Chinese National Healthy Living Centre in London, set up the Chinese Takeaway Project. The aim of the project was to improve the nutritional knowledge of takeaway cooks while reinforcing the values of traditional healthy Chinese practices through free training sessions across the country. Training was conducted by Wynnie Chan, a Cantonese-speaking nutritionist, who emphasized the importance of better cooking methods, such as limiting the use of fat and salt, eliminating MSG and food colourings and encouraging the use of more fruit and vegetables and leaner cuts of meat. The development of healthier versions of popular Chinese takeaway dishes, such as sweet and sour pork, chicken chow mein, aromatic crispy duck and beef in black bean sauce, meant that these and other healthier options became available in many takeaway shops. In addition, by using better cooking practices and healthier ingredients, takeaway food was brought closer to its true source.

Here is a book that contains simple-to-follow recipes with details of the nutritional content of each recipe, such as the amount of fat, calories and sodium. This means that you can plan and choose dishes that fit in with your lifestyle, whether you are someone who wants to lose weight, a busy mother who needs to feed her family quick, healthy meals or someone who just loves eating Chinese food. What could be better?

INTRODUCTION

The press portrays two very different views of Chinese food – some claim that it is unhealthy because it is full of fat, salt and MSG, while others believe that the Chinese diet is healthy and nutritious because it uses lots of vegetables and a minimum of oil. Whichever school of belief you support, the aim of this book is to show you that Chinese food, if cooked properly, can be healthy and delicious. Food should be enjoyed and eating a balanced diet is important for preventing disease and maintaining health.

Traditionally, the Chinese diet was based around vegetables and grain foods, such as rice and noodles, with meats and high-fat foods used as garnishes and flavourings rather than as the main ingredients. There is increasing scientific evidence to show that this type of low-fat, high-fibre diet is very beneficial to maintaining a healthy lifestyle, as it is linked to a lower risk of obesity, heart disease, diabetes and some cancers.

As countries have become more industrialized and Westernized, the proportions of foods that we eat have changed so that we now have an overemphasis on foods that are high in fat, salt and protein. The recipes in *Fresh Chinese* aim to redress some of the imbalance by bringing things back to basics, reducing the amount of salt, fat and sugar while increasing the amount of fruit and vegetables in most dishes – and all without compromising on taste.

WYNNIE CHAN

The Chinese National Healthy Living Centre in London has been active in promoting the health of both the Chinese and British population in the UK through a range of initiatives. The Chinese Healthy Takeaway Project is one such initiative, co-funded by the British Heart Foundation, the New Opportunities Fund and the Chinese Takeaway Association. This project aims to teach chefs across the UK the principles of healthy cooking, to reinforce traditional good cooking practices and encourage healthier alternatives to standard items on their menus.

EDDIE CHAN, DIRECTOR,

CHINESE NATIONAL HEALTHY LIVING CENTRE, UK

EATING FOR GOOD HEALTH

Foods are divided into five main groups, and a balanced diet is based on eating foods from each group in the right proportions.

THE FIVE FOOD GROUPS

These are breads, cereals and potatoes; fruit and vegetables; milk and dairy foods; meat, fish and other sources of protein; and sources of sugar and fat.

BREAD, CEREALS AND POTATOES This group is rich in starchy carbohydrates and includes breakfast cereals, rice, pasta, noodles, yam and oats. It should form the basis of most of your meals. Foods in this group are rich sources of insoluble fibre, calcium, iron and B vitamins, which keep your gut, bones and blood healthy. Try to eat wholegrain, wholemeal or high-fibre versions.

FRUIT AND VEGETABLES This group is an important source of antioxidants, such as vitamin C and beta-carotene (the vegetable equivalent of vitamin A), which help protect us from life-threatening diseases such as

cancers and heart disease. Fruits and vegetables are also rich in soluble fibre, which can help to reduce blood cholesterol. Try to include five portions of fruit and vegetables each day – they do not all have to be fresh or organic, although that is ideal, and can include frozen, canned and dried versions, as well as juices.

A portion of fruit is equivalent to:

1 slice of a very large fruit, e.g., melon, mango or pineapple | 1 avocado or grapefruit | 1 medium fruit, e.g., banana, pear, apple or orange | 2 small fruits, e.g., clementines, apricots, kiwi fruit or plums | 1 cup of very small fruit, e.g., grapes or strawberries | 2–3 tablespoons of canned fruit in natural unsweetened juice, e.g., lychees or peaches | 1 tablespoon of dried fruit, e.g., raisins or dates | 150 ml (¼ pint) of fresh fruit juice

A portion of vegetables is equivalent to:

2 tablespoons of broccoli, Chinese leaves, courgettes, spinach, cabbage, carrots, sweetcorn, shiitake mushrooms or pak choi | 1 dessert bowlful of salad | 1 cupful of sprouted beans | 150 ml (¼ pint) of fresh vegetable juice

MILK AND DAIRY FOODS This group provides essential nutrients, such as calcium and protein, as well as vitamins A, D and B12, which are important for maintaining the health of your bones, skin and blood. Try to include a couple of servings from this group every day and choose low-fat options if possible. Chinese people (except those in northern regions of China) do not generally include dairy foods in their everyday diet. Their main sources of calcium are tofu, bony fish, green leafy vegetables and calcium-fortified soya milk.

MEAT, FISH AND PROTEIN ALTERNATIVES The nutrients supplied by this food group include iron, protein, B vitamins and magnesium, which are needed to maintain healthy blood and efficient functioning of the immune system. Choose a maximum of two servings each day from: lean red meat, fish, chicken, turkey, eggs, nuts, beans and pulses. Beans and pulses, such as black-eye beans, mung beans, broad beans and lentils, make great protein alternatives, as do tofu and beancurd.

FOODS CONTAINING SUGAR AND FOODS CONTAINING FAT Try to keep foods such as savoury snacks, biscuits, cakes, crisps, pastries, sweets, chocolate, pies, butter and carbonated drinks to a minimum, as these contain high levels of fat and/or refined sugar. They are therefore high in calories and can hinder your efforts to lose weight. They also often contain additives such as artificial flavouring, colouring and preservatives, which are harmful and upset the body's natural balance.

Tips to reduce the amount of fat in your diet:
ONE Choose leaner cuts of meat whenever you can – for example, buy pork loin instead of belly pork. **TWO** Trim any visible fat from meat and poultry either before or after cooking – for example, remove the skin from chicken and duck. **THREE** Steam foods instead of frying or deep-frying them. **FOUR** Skim the fat from the surface of stocks and sauces made from meat or poultry.

FIVE Cut down on the amount of oil you use for stir-frying. One tablespoon of oil is more than enough when stir-frying a meal for four. **SIX** Always use a spoon to measure oil rather than pouring it directly from a bottle. This way you will know exactly how much you are using. **SEVEN** Use a nonstick sauté or griddle pan so you can cut down on the amount of oil you use. **EIGHT** Choose low-fat versions of products when available – for example, reduced-fat coconut milk, peanut butter or soya milk.

WHAT ABOUT SUGAR?

Although all fruit and vegetables contain natural sugars, it is the refined sugars that are hidden in many foods, from squashes to ready-made meals, which can cause particular problems. Often we do not realize how much sugar we are consuming, so be aware of how much sugar bought food products may contain by checking the list of ingredients on the packet. Ideally, cook your own meals using natural ingredients.

Tips to reduce the amount of sugar in your diet:
ONE Choose sugar-free or low-calorie fruit squashes. **TWO** Experiment by cutting down on the amount of

sugar you add to your marinades or in cooking. **THREE** Reduced-sugar and low-sugar foods can be helpful aids in the kitchen – for example, choose fruit that has been canned in its natural juice rather than in syrup. **FOUR** Choose fresh fruit for dessert rather than a sticky, sweet pudding.

WHAT ABOUT SALT?

While we all need a small amount of salt (sodium chloride) for our body to function efficiently, as a nation we are consuming far too much. Recent scientific studies among the adult population have shown that a high level of salt is associated with high blood pressure or hypertension and that people suffering from high blood pressure are three times more likely to develop heart disease and strokes.

Tips to reduce the amount of salt in your diet:

ONE Flavour foods with herbs and spices, such as ginger, garlic, coriander, Szechuan peppercorns, star anise, spring onions, chilli and lemon grass, instead of salt. **TWO** Limit the amount of bottled sauces you use – for example, soy sauce, yellow bean sauce or hoisin sauce. If you're used to using a heaped tablespoon of oyster sauce on your vegetables, you can easily reduce the amount simply by levelling off the tablespoon, and you probably won't even notice the difference. **THREE** Stock cubes contain salt and some also contain monosodium glutamate as a flavour enhancer. Whenever possible make your own stocks and use these to enhance and enrich the taste of foods. This will also help you to reduce the amount of salt and bottled sauces you use in your cooking. Freezing small quantities of homemade stock in freezer bags ensures that you will always have an emergency supply without having to resort to a packet. **FOUR** Don't add salt to the cooking water for vegetables or rice – you don't need it. If you want to, you can use stock instead. **FIVE** Japanese Tamari sauce is much more concentrated than Chinese soy sauce, which means that you need to use only a small amount. Low-sodium alternatives, such as Shoyu sauce or low-sodium salt can be helpful but should be avoided by people with diabetes and kidney disease because they contain too much potassium. **SIX** Choose unsalted nuts or wipe excess salt off salted nuts with absorbent kitchen paper before using them in cooking. **SEVEN** Don't automatically add salt to a dish before you have tasted it to see if it needs extra flavouring.

EQUIPMENT

The right equipment will make it much easier for you to cook authentic Chinese meals. Chinese supermarkets are a great place to stock up on the following.

NONSTICK SAUTE PAN This is ideal for stir-frying and should preferably be at least 30 cm (12 inches) in diameter. I prefer this type of pan to a wok when low-fat cooking because the temperature from an electric hob or gas ring often isn't high enough to properly heat the sides of the wok. It then takes much longer than it should to stir-fry your food because it is competing for a small amount of cooking space at the bottom of the wok.

NONSTICK GRIDDLE PAN This is useful for cooking meats and fish and will allow you to use a minimal amount of oil.

NONSTICK SPATULA OR WOODEN SPOON Perfect for both stir-frying and mixing.

PAIR OF LONG WOODEN CHOPSTICKS These are very versatile and can be used for mixing, stir-frying or serving food.

WOK WITH A LID AND WOK RACK FOR STEAMING A large wok is best – preferably at least 30 cm (12 inches) in diameter.

BAMBOO STEAMERS These should have a diameter of at least 25 cm (10 inches) – smaller ones look lovely but aren't very practical if you're cooking for a family.

STEAMERS are ideal for cooking dumplings and buns, but you'll need to line the bottom with greaseproof paper to prevent the food from sticking.

LIDDED SAUCEPANS These can be used for cooking rice or stock.

STAINLESS STEEL KNIVES OR A CLEAVER Used for chopping and cutting meat and vegetables.

CHINA CHINESE RICE BOWLS, CHOPSTICKS AND CHINESE SPOONS Chinese eating is a social affair with the diners helping themselves to food from communal dishes in the centre of the table. Go for authenticity – you can't truly enjoy Chinese food if you eat it with a knife and fork off your own plate!

STORE CUPBOARD INGREDIENTS

The recipes in this book are simple to follow and mostly use ingredients that are readily available from good supermarkets and specialist Oriental stores. If you keep a supply of the store-cupboard essentials listed below you will find it quick and easy to prepare delicious Chinese meals with authentic ingredients.

RICE OR FAAN This is a staple food in southern China and forms the basis of most meals. For long grain choose Thai Jasmine rice or brown rice. For short grain use either glutinous rice or Japanese sushi rice.

NOODLES These can be bought fresh or dried. Fun noodles are made from rice flour – for example, rice noodles. Mein noodles are made from wheat flour with or without the addition of egg, buckwheat or shrimps – for example, wholewheat noodles, egg noodles or soba (Japanese buckwheat) noodles. (Cellophane or beanthread noodles aren't actually made from rice or wheat flours but from mung beans. For this reason they tend not to be used as a staple, as they are less nutritious.)

OILS Traditionally, peanut or groundnut oil is used in Chinese cooking, but these have a high saturated fat content. Olive and rapeseed oil contain less saturated fat and a higher proportion of 'good' fats. Both types of oil are promoted in diets for healthy hearts because they contain a higher proportion of monounsaturated fats, which have been shown in some scientific studies to help lower blood cholesterol. In addition, rapeseed oil has a higher proportion of omega-3 essential fats, which are believed to help to reduce the risk of heart disease. Sesame oil, which is made from roasted white sesame seeds, is often used in Chinese cooking.

CANNED FRUITS AND VEGETABLES Canned fruits and vegetables, such as mango, lychees, bamboo shoots and waterchestnuts, are versatile and easy to use for quick suppers and snacks.

LOW-FAT ALTERNATIVES Low-fat or reduced-fat coconut milk and peanut butter are now available in most large supermarkets and food stores and they usually contain at least 25 per cent less fat than the original versions. They are ideal for people who want to reduce the amount of fat in their diet without sacrificing taste and flavour.

DRIED CHINESE MUSHROOMS These are relatively expensive, but a little goes a long way because they swell up once they've been reconstituted.

CORNFLOUR This is made from the starch of maize (corn) and is used as a thickener. Some people prefer to use potato starch as a thickening agent.

TOFU OR BEANCURD These can either be bought fresh from Oriental supermarkets or in long-life packs. They are available in two types: soft and firm. Firm is best for stir-frying, braising and roasting; the soft variety tends to be used for making sweet desserts, drinks and dressings.

HERBS AND SPICES Chilli, garlic, ginger, spring onions, coriander, shallots, lemon grass, Thai basil leaves, five spice powder, whole Szechuan peppercorns, peppercorns, star anise, sesame seeds, fennel seeds, ground cumin, bay leaves, cinnamon sticks, kaffir lime leaves and tamarind paste are ideal for enhancing the taste of foods in marinades or in stir-fries so that you don't need to add extra salt.

BOTTLED SAUCES Oyster sauce, hoisin sauce, black bean sauce and yellow bean sauce are useful for imparting distinct Chinese flavours to a dish. Sesame paste is often used to liven up cold dishes. Shoyu is a Japanese soy sauce, which contains less sodium (salt) than Chinese soy sauce. Tamari sauce is also a Japanese soy sauce that is less salty than the Chinese variety and has a richer, sweeter taste. Japanese soy sauces are brewed for longer and are made from roasted soya beans, wheat and salt.

Fish sauce is made from fermented salted anchovies or from shrimps. It is an acquired taste and tends to be very salty and so should be used in only very small quantities.

VINEGAR Balsamic, rice wine or red vinegar gives food an extra pungency. Chinese red vinegar is less acidic and is often used as a dip. Alternatively, you can dilute Balsamic vinegar with equal quantities of stock or water to make a dip.

WRAPPERS Dried rice paper sheets are a useful store cupboard ingredient. Wonton skins can be bought fresh and kept in the fridge for about five days or you can freeze them for later use (they are best frozen on the same day you buy them).

CHINESE RICE WINE Rice wine (preferably Shaohsing) is often used as a marinade or cooking ingredient in stir-fries. Dry sherry is an acceptable alternative.

BEANS, LENTILS, NUTS AND SEEDS Dried, frozen or canned pulses and beans make excellent protein alternatives to meat, as do nuts and seeds. They are all useful for livening up plain rice, noodles or salads.

FRESH FRUIT AND VEGETABLES Popular vegetables include bok choi (pak choi), Chinese leaves, Chinese flowering cabbage (choi sum), Chinese mustard greens (kai lan), beansprouts, Chinese flowering chives and baby sweetcorn. Fruits include mango, lychees, star fruit (carambola), kumquats, kiwifruit, bananas, physalis and papaya.

MENU PLANS

AMILY MENU FOR 4–6 PEOPLE

Beef and tomato *(see page 75)*

Sesame salmon with shredded
  vegetables *(see page 125)*

Bamboo shoots, straw mushrooms
  and broccoli *(see page 204)*

Vegetable chop suey *(see page 194)*

Boiled rice *(see page 224)*

Platter of oranges

**FAMILY VEGETARIAN MENU
FOR 4–6 PEOPLE**

Fu yung with vegetables
  (see page 188)

Lentils with lemon grass and lime
  leaves *(see page 180)*

Stir-fried tofu with assorted
  vegetables *(see page 176)*

Sesame broccoli *(see page 169)*

Boiled rice *(see page 224)*

Sliced melon

**TAKEAWAY MENU A
FOR 4–6 PEOPLE**

Chicken and creamed sweetcorn
  soup *(see page 54)*

Beef with black bean sauce
  (see page 70)

Sweet and sour pork *(see page 82)*

Vegetable chop suey *(see page 194)*

Vegetable fried rice *(see page 226)*

Sesame bananas *(see page 248)*

**TAKEAWAY MENU B
FOR 4–6 PEOPLE**

Hot and sour soup *(see page 60)*

King prawns with ginger and spring
  onions *(see page 126)*

Spare ribs *(see page 86)*

Chicken and cashew nuts with
  vegetables *(see page 113)*

Boiled rice *(see page 224)*

Lychees

ROMANTIC MENU FOR 2 PEOPLE

Prawn and grapefruit salad
  (use ½ quantities) *(see page 48)*

Oysters with black bean sauce
  (use ½ quantities) *(see page 132)*

Duck and pineapple (use ½
  quantities) *(see page 104)*

Chilli kale (use ½ quantities)
  (see page 168)

Boiled rice (2 bowls) *(see page 224)*

Strawberries

BUFFET MENU FOR 8–10 PEOPLE

Sesame prawn toasts *(see page 46)*

Fresh spring rolls *(see page 36)*

Chandoori chicken *(see page 100)*

Pork satay *(see page 91)*

Sweet and sour prawns
  (see page 135)

Sesame broccoli *(see page 169)*

Roasted tofu with Szechuan relish
  (see page 186)

Steamed buns *(see page 223)*

Almond jelly with assorted fruits
  (see page 240)

**SPECIAL BANQUET MENU
FOR 8–10 PEOPLE**

Minty carrot and kohlrabi salad
  (see page 47)

Crispy aromatic duck *(see page 32)*

Sea bass with spring onion and
  ginger dressing *(see page 150)*

Garlic steamed prawns
  (see page 130)

Roast pork *(see page 84)*

Stir-fried bok choi with shiitake
  mushrooms *(see page 178)*

Sea-spiced aubergines
  (see page 196)

Stir-fried noodles with peanuts
  and sweetcorn
(see page 210)

Boiled rice *(see page 224)*

Tropical fruit platter *(see page 246)*

STOCKS

Stocks are an important part of Chinese cooking and making your own is the best way to impart great flavours without adding unnecessary salt, MSG or artificial additives. Make stock in bulk and then freeze in smaller amounts so that you always have some handy when you are cooking. It is so versatile and can be used in soups, stews and stir-fries.

CHICKEN STOCK

INGREDIENTS 1.5 kg (3 lb) chicken bones | 1 kg (2 lb) skinless chicken thighs and legs | 3.5 litres (6 pints) water | 2 spring onions | 2 slices fresh ginger

ONE Put the chicken bones into a large saucepan with the meat. **TWO** Add the water and bring to the boil. Turn down the heat to a simmer and remove any scum that rises to the top. Add the spring onions and ginger and simmer, partially covered, for 3–4 hours. **THREE** Leave the stock to cool slightly, then strain and pour into a container, cover and store in the refrigerator until ready to use. The stock will keep for 2 days. Before using, skim any fat from the top of the stock.

Makes about 3 litres (5 pints)

BEEF STOCK

INGREDIENTS 1.75 kg (3½ lb) beef bones | 1.5 kg (3 lb) lean braising steak, cut into pieces | 5 litres (9 pints) water | 125 g (4 oz) onions, cut into chunks | 4 large carrots, cut into chunks | 3–4 slices fresh root ginger | 2 cinnamon sticks | 2 star anise

ONE Put the beef bones and pieces into a large saucepan with the meat. **TWO** Add the water and bring it to the boil. Turn down the heat to a simmer and remove any scum that rises to the top. **THREE** Add the onions, carrots, ginger, cinnamon and star anise and simmer, partially covered, for 4 hours. **FOUR** Leave the stock to cool slightly, then strain and pour into a container. Cover and store in the refrigerator until ready to use. It will keep for 2 days. Before using, skim any fat from the top.

Makes about 2.5 litres (4 pints)

PORK STOCK

INGREDIENTS 1.75 kg (4 lb) pork bones │ 1.5 kg (3 lb) lean pork shoulder or leg, cut into pieces │ 5 litres (9 pints) water │ 125 g (4 oz) onions, cut into chunks │ 4 large carrots, cut into chunks │ 3–4 slices fresh root ginger

ONE Put the pork bones into a large saucepan with the meat. **TWO** Add the water and bring to the boil. Turn down the heat to simmer and remove any scum that rises to the top. Add the onions, carrots and ginger and simmer, partially covered, for 4 hours. **THREE** Leave the stock to cool slightly, then strain and pour into a container. Cover and store the stock in the refrigerator until ready to use. The stock will keep for 2 days. Before using, skim any fat from the top.

Makes about 2.5 litres (4 pints)

VEGETABLE STOCK

INGREDIENTS 1 kg (2 lb) Chinese leaves | 1 kg (2 lb) leeks | 1 kg (2 lb) carrots | 1 kg (2 lb) onions | 4 slices fresh root ginger | 4 bay leaves | 4.5 litres (8 pints) water

ONE Put the vegetables into a large saucepan with the ginger and bay leaves. **TWO** Add the water and bring to the boil. Turn down the heat to simmer, then cover the pan and simmer for 2 hours. **THREE** Leave the stock to cool slightly, then strain and pour into a container. Cover and store in the refrigerator until ready to use. It will keep for 2 days.

Makes about 2.5 litres (4 pints)

FISH STOCK

INGREDIENTS 500 g (1 lb) fish bones | 250 g (8 oz) leeks | 250 g (8 oz) onions | 250 g (8 oz) celery | 250 g (8 oz) carrots | 2.5 litres (4 pints) water | handful of mixed herbs, e.g., coriander, parsley, spring onions | 2 bay leaves | 1 tablespoon white peppercorns

ONE Wash the fish bones and put them into a large saucepan. **TWO** Peel and roughly chop the vegetables. **THREE** Add the water and bring to the boil, then turn down the heat to simmer. Remove any scum that rises to the top. Add the vegetables, herbs and peppercorns and cook, partially covered, for 1½ hours. **FOUR** Leave the stock to cool slightly, then strain and pour into a container. Cover and store in the refrigerator for up to 24 hours until ready to use.

Makes about 1.8 litres (3 pints)

LEMON AND FISH SAUCE

INGREDIENTS 2 red chillies, deseeded and chopped | ½ garlic clove, crushed | 60 ml (2 fl oz) fresh lemon juice | 60 ml (2 fl oz) Thai fish sauce | 3 tablespoons light muscovado sugar | 125 ml (4 fl oz) water

ONE Mix together all the ingredients in a bowl. **TWO** Transfer to a screw-top jar. This sauce will keep in the refrigerator for a week.

Makes about 275 ml (9 fl oz)

NUTRIENT ANALYSIS PER 15 ML SERVING 41 kJ – 10 kcal – 0.2 g protein – 2.5 g carbohydrate – 2.0 g sugars – 0 g fat – 0 g saturates – 0 g fibre – 235 mg sodium

LIME AND SESAME DRESSING

INGREDIENTS 3 tablespoons toasted sesame seeds │ 1 tablespoon shoyu or tamari sauce │ 75 ml (3 fl oz) fresh lime juice │ 2 tablespoons rapeseed or extra virgin olive oil │ 1 teaspoon Worcestershire sauce

ONE Whizz all the ingredients in a blender until thick and creamy. **TWO** Pour into a screw-top jar and chill in the refrigerator until ready to use. This dressing will keep for about 1 week in the refrigerator.

Makes 250 ml (8 fl oz)

NUTRIENT ANALYSIS PER 15 ML SERVING 58 kJ – 14 kcal – 0.2 g protein – 0.1 g carbohydrate – 0.1 g sugars – 1.4 g fat – 0.2 g saturates – 0.1 g fibre – 19 mg sodium

TOFU AND MIRIN DRESSING

INGREDIENTS 2 tablespoons mirin (Japanese rice wine) | 2 tablespoons rice vinegar | 1 tablespoon shoyu or tamari sauce | 1 tablespoon chopped fresh root ginger | 75 g (3 oz) silken soft tofu | 75 g (3 oz) carrots, chopped

ONE Whizz the mirin, rice vinegar, shoyu sauce, ginger and tofu in a blender. Stir in the carrots. **TWO** This dressing can be stored in the refrigerator for a couple of days.

Makes about 175 ml (6 fl oz)

NUTRIENT ANALYSIS PER 15 ML SERVING 27 kJ – 6 kcal – 0.5 g protein – 0.6 g carbohydrate – 0.4 g sugars – 0.2 g fat – 0 g saturates – 0.1 g fibre – 33 mg sodium

CHILLI DIPPING SAUCE

INGREDIENTS 2 teaspoons cornflour | 250 ml (8 fl oz) Vegetable Stock *(see page 21)* | 125 ml (4 fl oz) rice wine vinegar | 2 tablespoons shoyu or tamari sauce | 1 tablespoon soft brown sugar | 2 garlic cloves, crushed | 1 slice fresh root ginger, peeled and finely chopped | 1 red chilli, deseeded and finely chopped

ONE Combine the cornflour and stock in a small saucepan and stir until dissolved. **TWO** Stir in the wine vinegar, shoyu sauce, sugar, garlic, ginger and chilli. Bring the sauce to the boil, stirring constantly until it has thickened. **THREE** Remove the pan from the heat and leave to cool, then spoon the sauce into a serving bowl. Use immediately.

Makes about 300 ml (½ pint)

NUTRIENT ANALYSIS PER 15 ML SERVING 23 kJ – 5.5 cal – 0.1 g protein – 1.2 g carbohydrate – 0.6 g sugars – 0 g fat – 0 g saturates – 0 g fibre – 34 mg sodium

PINEAPPLE DIPPING SAUCE

INGREDIENTS 1 tablespoon rice wine vinegar | juice of 1 lemon | 1 teaspoon brown sugar | 1 garlic clove, crushed | 2 red chillies, deseeded and sliced | 125 g (4 oz) crushed pineapple, fresh or canned in juice

ONE Mix the vinegar, lemon juice, sugar, garlic and chillies in a bowl. **TWO** Add the crushed pineapple and mix thoroughly. Serve immediately.

Serves 4

NUTRIENT ANALYSIS PER 15 ML SERVING 32 kJ – 7.3 kcal – 0.1 g protein – 1.8 g carbohydrate – 1.8 g sugars – 0 g fat – 0 g saturates – 0.1 g fibre – trace sodium

SOUPS AND

STARTERS

CRISPY AROMATIC DUCK

This dish comes from Szechuan where, traditionally, marinated duck is steamed then deep-fried until crisp and golden. In this recipe, the duck is also cooked first, essentially to tenderize the meat so that it comes away from the bones easily. It is then grilled rather than deep-fried to cut down the fat content.

INGREDIENTS 1 x 1 kg (2 lb) Gressingham duck, halved and flattened slightly | 3 litres (5 pints) Vegetable Stock *(see page 21)*

MARINADE 1 tablespoon five spice powder | 1 tablespoon ground ginger | 2 star anise | 2 tablespoons Szechuan peppercorns | 2 tablespoons black peppercorns | 3 tablespoons cumin seeds | 3 tablespoons fennel seeds | 1 tablespoon shoyu or tamari sauce | 6 slices fresh root ginger, peeled and crushed | 6 spring onions, chopped | 2 bay leaves, crumbled

TO SERVE Chinese Pancakes | sliced cucumber | sliced spring onions | hoisin sauce diluted with stock

ONE Combine the marinade ingredients and rub into the duck halves. Cover and leave overnight or for at least a couple of hours in the refrigerator. **TWO** Bring the stock to the boil in a large saucepan. Gently lower the duck into the pan, then bring the stock back to the boil. Turn down the heat to low, cover the pan and simmer for 45 minutes. **THREE** Leave the duck to cool in the liquid for 10–15 minutes then remove it with a slotted spoon and pat dry on kitchen paper. **FOUR** Place the duck halves skin-side up on a rack set in a roasting tin. Put the tin under a preheated very hot grill and grill for about 3–5 minutes to brown the skin. Watch closely. **FIVE** Remove the duck and blot the excess fat from the skin. Leave the duck to cool slightly then flake the meat with 2 forks. **SIX** Serve with Chinese pancakes, sliced cucumber, sliced spring onions and some hoisin sauce diluted with a little stock.

Serves 8 as a starter

NUTRIENT ANALYSIS PER SERVING 1750 kJ – 423 kcal – 20.0 g protein – 0 g carbohydrate – 0 g sugars – 38.1 g fat – 11.4 g saturates – 0 g fibre – 129 mg sodium

HEALTHY TIP Duck skin is high in fat, but this recipe wouldn't be what it is if the skin were removed. Some fat will be lost as part of the simmering process, yet more can be removed by blotting the duck with absorbent paper after grilling.

recipe illustrated on pages 34–35

FRESH SPRING ROLLS

Deep-fried spring rolls are a firm favourite at Chinese restaurants and takeaways. This version is adapted from a Vietnamese recipe and uses soft rice paper sheets stuffed with fresh herbs and crunchy vegetables and dipped in a tasty lemony sauce.

INGREDIENTS 8 x 22 cm (8½ inches) round dried rice paper sheets │ Lemon and Fish Sauce *(see page 23)*, **for dipping**

FILLING 6 Chinese dried mushrooms │ 50 g (2 oz) thin rice noodles │ 250 g (8 oz) fresh beansprouts │ 1 small cucumber, cut into strips │ 2 tablespoons roughly torn fresh mint leaves │ 2 tablespoons roughly torn fresh coriander leaves │ 1 carrot, grated │ 2 tablespoons roasted unsalted peanuts, coarsely chopped

ONE Put the dried mushrooms in a heatproof bowl, cover with boiling water and put a plate on top to keep the steam in. Set aside for 20–30 minutes or until soft. Drain the mushrooms, discard the stalks and squeeze the water from the caps, then shred them finely. **TWO** Place the rice noodles in a bowl, pour over some boiling water and leave to stand, covered, for about 10 minutes. Drain the noodles, rinse with cold water and set aside. **THREE** Soak the sheets of rice paper in a bowl of warm water, one at a time, for about 30–60 seconds until softened, then place on a clean, dry tea towel. **FOUR** To prepare the spring rolls, put a little of all the filling ingredients on each rice paper sheet, roll up the bottom half of the rice paper, fold in the sides and roll over to enclose the filling. **FIVE** The spring rolls can be prepared about 20–30 minutes before serving. Cover them with clingfilm and place in the refrigerator until required. Serve the spring rolls with the Lemon and Fish Sauce.

Makes 8, serves 4 as a starter

NUTRIENT ANALYSIS PER ROLL 290 kJ – 70 kcal – 2.7 g protein – 8.8 g carbohydrate – 1.4 g sugars – 2.7 g fat – 0.5 g saturates – 0.8 g fibre – 45 mg sodium

HEALTHY TIP You can use a wide variety of different coloured vegetables as fillings for these spring rolls. Not only will they look attractive and appetizing, but they will also ensure that you meet your daily requirements for a wide range of phyto-nutrients.

PAN-FRIED DUMPLINGS

Also known as potstickers, these dumplings are popular among people from the north of China who sometimes eat them as a main meal. Here they are pan-fried but they can also be boiled or steamed.

INGREDIENTS 300 g (10 oz) strong plain flour | 250 ml (8 fl oz) hot water | 1 tablespoon rapeseed oil | 120 ml (4 fl oz) water

FILLING 100 g (3½ oz) courgettes, thinly shredded | 200 g (7 oz) chicken, minced | 1 spring onion, thinly sliced | 1 tablespoon finely minced fresh root ginger | 1 teaspoon Chinese rice wine or dry sherry | ½ teaspoon freshly ground black pepper | 2 tablespoons shoyu or tamari sauce

ONE Prepare the dough. Sift the flour into a mixing bowl. Slowly add the water to form a ball, then knead for a couple of minutes until the dough is smooth. Cover the bowl with a damp towel or clingfilm and leave at room temperature for about 30 minutes. **TWO** Mix together all the ingredients for the filling. **THREE** Working on a lightly floured surface, roll the dough into a long cylinder about 1.5 cm (¾ inch) in diameter and cut it into about 18 pieces each 1 cm (½ inch) long. Cover the dough with clingfilm to stop it drying out and use a narrow rolling pin to roll out each piece into a circle about 7 cm (3 inches) in diameter. The centre should be slightly thicker than the edge. **FOUR** Place a heaped teaspoon of filling in the centre of each wrapper and pinch tightly to seal the edges, so that it looks like a Cornish pasty. **FIVE** Heat a large lidded nonstick sauté pan until hot. Add the oil and swirl to cover the bottom of the pan. Lower the heat to medium and add the dumplings, making sure that there is a slight gap between each one. Turn the heat up to high, then add the water, cover with the lid and cook for about 10 minutes or until the water has almost evaporated. Remove the lid and cook for another couple of minutes until the bottom of the dumplings have turned golden brown. Serve the dumplings brown side up.

Makes about 18 dumplings

NUTRIENT ANALYSIS PER DUMPLING 284 kJ – 67 kcal – 4.5 g protein – 10.8 g carbohydrate – 0.3 g sugars – 1.0 g fat – 0.2 g saturates – 0.5 g fibre – 63 mg sodium

HEALTHY TIP Courgettes are low in calories and a good source of beta-carotene. They also contain some vitamin C and folate.

recipe illustrated on pages 40–41

LETTUCE WRAPS

Lettuce-wrapped minced chicken is a popular southern Chinese dish. This vegetarian version uses a mixture of vegetables and tofu to fill the leaves.

INGREDIENTS 6 dried Chinese mushrooms │ 1 tablespoon rapeseed or olive oil │ 4 garlic cloves, crushed │ 2 large shallots, sliced │ 2 slices fresh root ginger, chopped │ 2 fresh red chillies, deseeded and sliced │ 8 canned water chestnuts, diced │ 50 g (2 oz) canned bamboo shoots, diced │ 150 g (5 oz) carrots, diced │ 1 heaped tablespoon hoisin sauce │ 2 teaspoons shoyu or tamari sauce │ 1 x 349 g (11½ oz) pack silken firm tofu, diced │ 150 ml (5 fl oz) Vegetable Stock *(see page 21)* │ 1½ teaspoons cornflour │ 4 spring onions, sliced │ 50 g (2 oz) toasted walnut pieces │ freshly ground black pepper │ 2 Romaine or Cos lettuces, separated into leaves

ONE Put the dried mushrooms into a heatproof bowl, cover with boiling water and put a plate on top to keep the steam in. Set aside for 20–30 minutes or until soft. Drain the mushrooms, remove the stalks, then squeeze the water out of the caps and chop them roughly. **TWO** Heat the oil in a nonstick pan or wok over a high heat until piping hot, add the garlic, shallots, ginger and chillies and stir-fry for a couple of minutes. **THREE** Add the water chestnuts, bamboo shoots and carrots and stir-fry for about 5 minutes, then stir in the hoisin and shoyu sauces and season with black pepper. Add the tofu and stir gently to mix, then pour in the vegetable stock and bring to the boil. **FOUR** Meanwhile, dissolve the cornflour in a little water in a small bowl. Push the vegetables to the sides of the wok and pour the cornflour paste into the middle. When the sauce starts to thicken, bring in the surrounding mixture and mix well. **FIVE** Toss in the spring onions and walnuts. **SIX** To serve, take a lettuce leaf, spoon on some of the tofu vegetable mixture and fold it up into a neat parcel to eat.

Serves 4–6 as a starter

NUTRIENT ANALYSIS PER WRAP 1064 kJ – 250 kcal – 12.0 g protein – 17.2 g carbohydrate – 8.1 g sugars – 15.8 g fat – 1.7 g saturates – 3.3 g fibre – 181 mg sodium

HEALTHY TIP Walnuts contain a useful supply of the B vitamins thiamin and niacin. A recent study in the USA has shown that eating about 85 g (3½ oz) walnuts instead of saturated fats and as part of a general low-fat diet, can lower blood cholesterol levels. A high blood cholesterol level is linked to an increased risk of heart disease.

recipe illustrated on pages 44–45

SESAME PRAWN TOASTS

This low-fat baked variation of the traditionally deep-fried snack is quick and easy to make and uses French bread instead of sliced white bread.

INGREDIENTS 175 g (6 oz) raw prawns, roughly chopped │ ½ garlic clove, crushed │ ½ teaspoon grated fresh root ginger │ 1 small egg white, lightly beaten │ 1 spring onion, roughly chopped │ 1 teaspoon shoyu or tamari sauce │ 8 x 1.5 cm (¾ inch) slices crusty French bread │ 1 teaspoon rapeseed or olive oil │ 1 tablespoon toasted sesame seeds

ONE Whizz the prawns, garlic, ginger, egg white, spring onions and shoyu sauce to a paste in a food processor. Chill the prawn paste in the refrigerator for at least 20 minutes. **TWO** Toast the bread on one side, then lightly brush the untoasted side with oil. **THREE** Spread the prawn paste evenly over the toasted side of the bread and sprinkle the sesame seeds over the top. **FOUR** Place the toasts on an oven rack and cook in a preheated oven, 240°C (475°F), Gas Mark 9, for about 10 minutes or until the prawn paste is cooked and the toasts are crisp and browned.

Serves 4 as a starter

NUTRIENT ANALYSIS PER TOAST 492 kJ – 117 kcal – 7.6 g protein – 17.9 g carbohydrate – 1.1 g sugars – 2.1 g fat – 0.2 g saturates – 0.7 g fibre – 255 mg sodium

HEALTHY TIP Sesame seeds are an excellent source of protein. They also provide useful amounts of vitamin E, calcium and fibre.

MINTY CARROT AND KOHLRABI SALAD

In Cantonese cuisine pickled vegetables are always served in sweet and sour style. This combination is thought to help stimulate the appetite.

INGREDIENTS 250 g (8 oz) raw carrots, thinly sliced | 150 g (5 oz) raw kohlrabi, thinly sliced | 200 ml (7 fl oz) water | 65 ml (2½ fl oz) white wine vinegar | 1 tablespoon soft brown sugar | ½ teaspoon sea salt | 2 tablespoons chopped fresh mint leaves | 2 tablespoons chopped fresh coriander leaves

ONE Combine all the ingredients, apart from the mint and coriander, in a large bowl. Cover and refrigerate for about 1 hour, stirring occasionally. **TWO** To serve, drain the carrots and kohlrabi, and discard the pickling liquid. Rinse the vegetables in water. Place them in a serving bowl and toss with the mint and coriander leaves just before serving.

Serves 4 as a starter

NUTRIENT ANALYSIS PER SERVING 161 kJ – 39 kcal – 1.2 protein – 7.9 g carbohydrate – 7.3 g sugars – 0.3 g fat – 0.1 g saturates – 2.3 g fibre – 69 mg sodium

HEALTHY TIP Kohlrabi belongs to the brassica family, which includes cabbage, Brussels sprouts and broccoli. Many scientific studies have shown that these vegetables contain chemicals that can protect against some forms of cancer.

PRAWN AND GRAPEFRUIT SALAD

This dish comes from Thailand, where the pomelo is a common winter fruit. It looks like a gigantic yellow grapefruit with a slightly pointed top, but the flesh is drier and crisper than grapefruit.

INGREDIENTS 400 g (13 oz) large tiger prawns, raw or cooked, peeled and deveined | 2 large grapefruits or 1 large pomelo, peeled and segmented | 1 small red onion, thinly sliced | 1 small ripe avocado, chopped | 4 tablespoons Lemon and Fish Sauce *(see page 23)* | 1 tablespoon coriander leaves

ONE Bring a saucepan of water to the boil, add the prawns, if raw, and cook until they are pink, which will take 1–2 minutes. Remove the prawns with a slotted spoon and leave to cool. **TWO** Place the grapefruit segments, onion and avocado in a serving dish. Arrange the prawns on top and drizzle with the sauce. Toss to mix well. **THREE** Sprinkle with the coriander leaves and serve immediately.

Serves 4 as a starter

NUTRIENT ANALYSIS PER SERVING 766 kJ – 182 kcal – 19.7 g protein – 14.0 g carbohydrate – 13.2 g sugars – 5.7 g fat – 1.1 g saturates – 2.9 g fibre – 432 mg sodium

HEALTHY TIP Grapefruit and pomelo are excellent sources of vitamin C. The membranes contain some insoluble fibre called pectin, which helps to lower blood cholesterol levels.

CASHEW NUT AND VEGETABLE DUMPLINGS

INGREDIENTS 3 tablespoons glutinous rice flour | 275 g (9 oz) rice flour | 3 tablespoons arrowroot | 350 ml (12 fl oz) water | 1 tablespoon rapeseed or olive oil

FILLING 2 garlic cloves, crushed | 150 g (5 oz) bamboo shoots, finely chopped | 150 g (5 oz) carrots, finely grated | 200 g (7 oz) unsalted cashew nuts, roasted and roughly chopped | 2 spring onions, finely chopped | 2 tablespoons chopped fresh coriander leaves | 1 egg | 1 tablespoon cornflour | 1 tablespoon shoyu or tamari sauce | 1 teaspoon Thai fish sauce

ONE To make the pastry, put both kinds of rice flour in a saucepan with 1 tablespoon of the arrowroot, then stir in the water and oil. Cook over a medium heat, stirring constantly, until the mixture forms a ball and leaves the side of the pan clean. **TWO** Transfer the pastry to a mixing bowl and, while it's still firm, knead it for about 2–3 minutes until it is smooth and shiny. Cover with clingfilm until ready to use. **THREE** Mix all the ingredients for the filling in a large bowl. **FOUR** With your hands, roll the dough into small balls about 1 cm (½ inch) in diameter, then, with a small rolling pin, roll the dough into circles about 7 cm (3 inches) in diameter. **FIVE** Place a heaped tablespoon of filling in the centre of each wrapper. Fold over the sides to form semicircles and press the edges together. **SIX** Pour about 5 cm (2 inches) of water into a wok, place a metal or wooden rack in the wok and bring the water to boil. **SEVEN** Line the bottom of a bamboo steamer with greaseproof paper. **EIGHT** Place 8–10 dumplings in the bamboo steamer and put it on top of the wok rack. Cover and steam for 10–12 minutes or until the pastry is cooked and translucent. Check the water levels periodically and top up with hot water if necessary. Serve with Chilli Dipping Sauce *(see page 26)* or Pineapple Dipping Sauce *(see page 27)*.

Serves 8 as a starter or a light lunch

NUTRIENT ANALYSIS PER DUMPLING 1520 kJ – 364 kcal – 8.3 g protein – 49.7 g carbohydrate – 2.8 g sugars – 14.5 g fat – 3.0 g saturates – 1.7 g fibre – 134 mg sodium

recipe illustrated on pages 52–53

CHICKEN AND CREAMED SWEETCORN SOUP

INGREDIENTS 1.5 litres (2½ pints) Chicken Stock *(see page 18)* | 285 g (9½ oz) can creamed-style sweetcorn | 285 g (9½ oz) can sweetcorn kernels, drained | 100 g (3½ oz) cooked chicken, finely shredded | ½ teaspoon ground white pepper | 2 beaten eggs

CORNFLOUR PASTE 2 teaspoons cornflour mixed with 2 tablespoons chicken stock

ONE Bring the stock to the boil in a large saucepan, add the creamed-style sweetcorn and sweetcorn kernels and simmer for about 5 minutes. **TWO** Add the cooked chicken to the pan, then return the soup to the boil. Season with pepper and slowly stir in the cornflour paste. Turn off the heat. **THREE** Stirring continuously with a pair of chopsticks, slowly drizzle in the beaten eggs to form fine threads. Serve immediately.

Serves 4

NUTRIENT ANALYSIS PER SERVING 1048 kJ – 249 kcal – 14.3 g protein – 38.8 g carbohydrate – 6.8 g sugars – 5.6 g fat – 1.5 g saturates – 1.0 g fibre – 256 mg sodium

BUTTERNUT SQUASH AND TOFU SOUP

This recipe is so creamy and delicious that you might think it contains milk or cream. Pumpkin can be substituted for the butternut squash, if you like.

INGREDIENTS 1 large onion, roughly chopped │ 150 g (5 oz) carrots, cut into large chunks │ 1 butternut squash, weighing about 625–750 g (1¼–1½ lb), peeled and cut into large chunks │ 1 slice fresh root ginger │ 600 ml (1 pint) Vegetable Stock *(see page 21)* │ 250 g (8 oz) silken soft tofu, roughly chopped

ONE In a large saucepan, sweat the onion over a low heat for about 10 minutes. **TWO** Add the carrots, butternut squash, ginger and stock, then bring the mixture to the boil over a high heat. **THREE** Reduce the heat to low and simmer for about 25–30 minutes until all the vegetables are soft. **FOUR** Add the tofu, stir and bring the soup back to the boil over a medium heat. **FIVE** Pour the mixture into a food processor or blender and blend for about 30 seconds until the soup is smooth and creamy.

Serves 4–6

NUTRIENT ANALYSIS PER SERVING 611 kJ – 145 kcal – 8.0 g protein – 22.9 g carbohydrate – 14.3 g sugars – 3.1 g fat – 0.4 g saturates – 4.5 g fibre – 21 mg sodium

HEALTHY TIP Butternut squash is a good source of beta-carotene and vitamin E, both of which act as antioxidants, protecting the body against free radicals.

WONTON SOUP

Wontons are small dumplings that are often served in soup either on their own or with noodles; they are a very popular street food in oriental countries. Wonton wrappers can be found in the chiller cabinet in Chinese supermarkets and can be frozen, ideally on the day they are bought.

INGREDIENTS 45 wonton wrappers | 1.5 litres (2½ pints) Pork Stock *(see page 20)* **or** Chicken Stock *(see page 18)* | 8 Chinese leaves, shredded | spring onions, sliced

STUFFING 100 g (3½ oz) minced lean pork or chicken | 100 g (3½ oz) raw prawns, roughly chopped | 2 spring onions, finely sliced | 2 slices fresh root ginger, peeled and finely chopped | 75 g (3 oz) bamboo shoots, finely chopped | 1 egg white, lightly beaten | 1 tablespoon shoyu or tamari sauce | ½ teaspoon freshly ground black pepper | 1 teaspoon Chinese rice wine or dry sherry | 1 teaspoon sesame oil | 1 teaspoon cornflour

ONE Mix the ingredients for the stuffing thoroughly in a large bowl. **TWO** To wrap the wontons, place about ½ teaspoon of filling in the centre of each wonton wrapper. Brush 2 of the edges of the wrapper with water and fold over the wonton and seal to make a triangle. **THREE** Bring a large pan of water to the boil. Meanwhile, heat the stock in another saucepan and add the Chinese leaves. **FOUR** Gently lower a handful of wontons into the boiling water with a slotted spoon. Stir very gently to separate the wontons and make sure that they don't stick at the bottom of the pan. **FIVE** Bring the water back to the boil and cook the wontons, uncovered, for 5–6 minutes or until they are done and have floated to the surface. Transfer to a large serving bowl. **SIX** To serve, pour the stock and Chinese leaves over the wontons and sprinkle with the spring onions.

Serves 5–6 as a starter

NUTRIENT ANALYSIS PER SERVING 389 kJ – 92 kcal – 11.7 g protein – 8.0 g carbohydrate – 0.3 g sugars – 1.4 g fat – 0.4 g saturates – 0.2 g fibre – 203 mg sodium

HEALTHY TIP Traditionally, fatty pork is used for the wonton filling. Using lean pork or chicken makes the wontons lower in fat. Serve them with noodles and vegetables to make a complete low-fat light meal.

recipe illustrated on pages 58–59

HOT AND SOUR SOUP

This soup is found in both Szechuan and Peking cuisines. The traditional recipe calls for chicken's blood, but this vegetarian version is hot and pungent without being too overpowering.

INGREDIENTS 4 dried Chinese mushrooms │ 1.5 litres (2½ pints) Vegetable Stock *(see page 21)* │ 100 g (3½ oz) bamboo shoots, shredded │ 1 fresh red chilli, deseeded and sliced │ 125 g (4 oz) silken firm tofu, cubed │ 1 egg, lightly beaten

SEASONING 1 tablespoon sherry or rice wine │ 1 tablespoon white wine vinegar │ 1 tablespoon lime juice │ 1 teaspoon muscovado sugar │ 1 tablespoon dark soy sauce │ 1 teaspoon freshly ground black pepper

CORNFLOUR PASTE 2 tablespoons cornflour mixed with 4 tablespoons vegetable stock

TO SERVE 1 tablespoon chopped fresh coriander leaves │ 1 spring onion, sliced

ONE Put the dried mushrooms in a heatproof bowl, cover with boiling water and put a plate on top to keep the steam in. Set aside for 20–30 minutes. Drain the mushrooms and remove the stalks, squeeze the water out of the caps and chop them roughly. **TWO** Bring the stock to the boil in a large saucepan, add the Chinese mushrooms, bamboo shoots and chilli. **THREE** Stir in all the seasoning ingredients, then add the tofu and return the soup to the boil. **FOUR** Slowly stir in the cornflour paste to thicken the soup then bring it back to the boil again. **FIVE** Turn off the heat and stir in the beaten egg in a steady stream, stirring it round with a fork or a pair of chopsticks. **SIX** To serve, sprinkle with the coriander leaves and spring onions.

Serves 4

NUTRIENT ANALYSIS PER SERVING 1102 kJ – 262 kcal – 19.9 g protein – 32.2 g carbohydrate – 2.0 g sugars – 6.2 g fat – 1.6 g saturates – 0.50 g fibre – 202 mg sodium

HEALTHY TIP Capsaicin is the compound in chilli that gives it its heat. Studies have shown that chillies may help to lower blood pressure and blood cholesterol levels, and some people find chillies help to relieve blocked sinuses.

LEMON GRASS BROTH WITH TOFU AND MUSHROOMS

INGREDIENTS 1 litre (1¾ pints) Vegetable Stock *(see page 21)* | 2 lemon grass stalks, lightly crushed | 1 red chilli, chopped | 2 teaspoons shoyu or tamari sauce | pinch of white pepper | 200 g (7 oz) closed cap mushrooms, chopped | 250 g (8 oz) pack silken firm tofu, cubed | juice of ½ lime | handful of fresh basil leaves | 2 spring onions, sliced lengthways

ONE Bring the stock to the boil in a saucepan, add the lemon grass and red chilli, then leave to simmer for about 15–20 minutes, covered. **TWO** Season the broth with shoyu sauce and pepper. **THREE** Add the mushrooms and tofu and cook for 5–10 minutes. **FOUR** Add the lime juice, basil leaves and spring onions and stir gently. Serve immediately.

Serves 4 as an appetizer

NUTRIENT ANALYSIS PER SERVING 414 kJ – 99 kcal – 12.1 g protein – 1.3 g carbohydrate – 0.5 g sugars – 4.9 g fat – 0.9 g saturates – 0.7 g fibre – 479 mg sodium

HEALTHY TIP Tofu or beancurd is an excellent source of the plant hormone phyto-oestrogen. Research suggests that soya and soya products, such as tofu, can help to protect women against breast cancer and osteoporosis and may also help to alleviate the symptoms of the menopause.

MEAT

BEEF WITH GARLIC AND CHILLI SAUCE

INGREDIENTS 400 g (13 oz) sirloin beef, cut into 1 cm (½ inch) thick slices │ 1 teaspoon sesame oil

GARLIC AND CHILLI DIPPING SAUCE 2 garlic cloves, crushed │ 1 tablespoon shoyu or tamari sauce │ 1 teaspoon light muscovado sugar │ 2 red chillies, deseeded and finely chopped │ 1 tablespoon lime juice

ONE Beat the beef on both sides with a meat mallet to make it slightly thinner. **TWO** Brush the beef with the sesame oil and set aside. **THREE** Mix together all the ingredients for the dipping sauce in a small bowl and set aside. **FOUR** Place the beef on a preheated very hot griddle pan. For medium beef, cook for about 1½ minutes on each side until browned. Remove from the pan and let the beef rest for about 1 minute then slice thinly into 1 cm (½ inch) strips. **FIVE** Serve the beef with the dipping sauce and Sticky Rice *(see page 225)*.

Serves 4 with 2 other main dishes

NUTRIENT ANALYSIS PER SERVING 630 kJ – 150 kcal – 23.9 g protein – 1.9 g carbohydrate – 1.4 g sugars – 5.3 g fat – 2.1 g saturates – 0.1 g fibre – 196 mg sodium

HEALTHY TIP Beef is a valuable source of the minerals iron, zinc, manganese, selenium and chromium which help maintain health and growth.

SHREDDED BEEF WITH CARROTS AND CHILLI

INGREDIENTS 400 g (13 oz) rump steak, cut into thin strips, 6 cm (2½ inches) long | 2 tablespoons cornflour | 1 tablespoon rapeseed or olive oil | 2 garlic cloves, crushed | 2–3 fresh red chillies, deseeded and sliced | 400 g (13 oz) carrots, cut into thin strips, 6 cm (2½ inches) long | 2 teaspoons Chinese rice wine or dry sherry | 2 teaspoons rice wine vinegar | ½ tablespoon tomato ketchup | 1 teaspoon dark muscovado sugar | 2 teaspoons shoyu or tamari sauce | 3 spring onions, sliced, to garnish

ONE Put the beef strips in a bowl and mix in the cornflour. **TWO** Heat the oil in a nonstick sauté pan until piping hot, add the beef and fry for 1 minute on each side. Remove from the pan and set aside. **THREE** Add the garlic and chillies to the pan and stir-fry for a few seconds. Toss in the carrots, then add the rice wine, vinegar, ketchup, sugar and shoyu sauce and stir-fry for 1 more minute. **FOUR** Add the beef and mix with the carrot mixture. Serve garnished with the spring onion slices.

Serves 4 with 2 other main dishes

NUTRIENT ANALYSIS PER SERVING 953 kJ – 227 kcal – 23.1 g protein – 16.9 g carbohydrate – 9.1 g sugars – 7.3 g fat – 2.2 g saturates – 2.6 g fibre – 174 mg sodium

BEEF WITH BLACK BEAN SAUCE

This version of a popular Cantonese dish is cooked with beef stock, which makes the sauce rich and tasty without needing the addition of salt or monosodium glutamate (MSG). This is an excellent dish to serve with Stir-fried Bok Choi with Shiitake Mushrooms *(see page 178)*.

INGREDIENTS ½ tablespoon olive oil │ 1 tablespoon black bean sauce │ 400 g (13 oz) rump or fillet steak, sliced │ 1 red chilli, deseeded and cut into strips │ 100 g (3½ oz) onion, chopped in squares │ 300 g (10 oz) yellow peppers, cored, deseeded and chopped in squares │ 200 ml (7 fl oz) hot Beef Stock *(see page 19)*

CORNFLOUR PASTE 1 teaspoon cornflour mixed with 1 tablespoon water or stock

ONE Heat the oil in a nonstick sauté pan over a high heat until hot. Add the black bean sauce and stir-fry for a few seconds, then add the sliced beef and stir-fry for about 1 minute until half-cooked. **TWO** Mix in the chilli, onion and yellow peppers and stir-fry for about 1–2 minutes. **THREE** Add the hot stock and bring to the boil. **FOUR** Slowly stir in the cornflour paste until the sauce has thickened and become transparent. Serve immediately.

Serves 4 with 2 other main dishes

NUTRIENT ANALYSIS PER SERVING 817 kJ – 195 kcal – 23.6 g protein – 6.7 g carbohydrate – 3.7 g sugars – 8.4 g fat – 3.2 g saturates – 1.0 g fibre – 221 mg sodium

HEALTHY TIP Lean beef, such as fillet and rump steak, is an excellent source of iron, which is needed for healthy blood. Trimming excess visible fat ensures that this dish is low in fat.

recipe illustrated on pages 72–73

BEEF IN OYSTER SAUCE

This dish goes well with Sea Bass with Spring Onion and Ginger Dressing *(see page 150).* **Serve the two dishes as part of a family meal**.

INGREDIENTS 400 g (13 oz) mangetout | 1 tablespoon rapeseed or olive oil | 1 garlic clove, crushed | 500 g (1 lb) fillet steak, thinly sliced | 50 ml (2 fl oz) hot Beef Stock *(see page 19)* | 1 tablespoon oyster sauce

CORNFLOUR PASTE ½ tablespoon cornflour mixed with 2 tablespoons water

ONE Blanch the mangetout in a large pan of boiling water for 30 seconds, then remove with a slotted spoon and place on a serving dish. **TWO** Heat the oil in a nonstick sauté pan over a high heat, add the garlic and stir-fry for a few seconds until it is fragrant and beginning to brown. **THREE** Add the fillet steak and cook for 1 minute on each side. **FOUR** Add the hot stock and oyster sauce and mix thoroughly. Slowly stir in the cornflour paste and cook until the sauce thickens. **FIVE** Pour the beef mixture over the mangetout. Serve immediately.

Serves 4 with 2 other main dishes

NUTRIENT ANALYSIS PER SERVING 902 kJ – 215 kcal – 28.6 g protein – 8.4 g carbohydrate 3.4 g sugar – 7.6 g fat – 2.3 g saturates – 2.3 g fibre – 228 mg sodium

BEEF AND TOMATO

INGREDIENTS 1 teaspoon shoyu or tamari sauce | 2 teaspoons cornflour | 2 teaspoons Chinese rice wine or dry sherry | 500 g (1 lb) rump steak, thinly sliced | 1 tablespoon rapeseed or olive oil | 2 garlic cloves, sliced | 2 slices fresh root ginger, peeled and finely chopped | 500 g (1 lb) fresh tomatoes, preferably plum tomatoes | 50 ml (2 fl oz) Beef Stock *(see page 19)*

CORNFLOUR PASTE 1 teaspoon cornflour mixed with 1 tablespoon water

ONE Mix together the shoyu sauce, cornflour and rice wine and rub into the sliced beef. Set aside to marinate for 10 minutes. **TWO** Heat the oil in a nonstick sauté pan over a high heat until hot. Add the garlic and ginger and stir-fry for a few seconds. **THREE** Add the beef slices and stir-fry for 1 minute on each side. Remove and set aside. **FOUR** In the same pan, add the fresh tomatoes and cook over a medium heat for 1 minute, then add the beef stock. Turn the heat to low, cover the pan and simmer for 5 minutes. **FIVE** Return the beef slices to the pan and mix thoroughly, then add the cornflour paste, stirring continuously until the sauce has thickened and turned transparent.

Serves 4 with 2 other main dishes

NUTRIENT ANALYSIS PER SERVING 896 kJ – 213 kcal – 25.8 g protein – 9.9 g carbohydrate – 3.6 g sugar – 7.8 g fat – 2.4 g saturates – 1.2 g fibre – 123 mg sodium

SPICED BEEF AND VEGETABLE STEW

This recipe originates from Vietnam. Don't expect a thick stew from this recipe – it's more like a *pot au feu*. This dish goes well with steamed yam (steam peeled slices of yam over a high heat for 20 minutes) and Sesame Broccoli *(see page 169)*.

INGREDIENTS 1 tablespoon rapeseed or olive oil │ 1 large onion, chopped │ 4 slices fresh root ginger, peeled and roughly chopped │ 2 fresh chillies, deseeded and sliced │ 500 g (1 lb) lean braising or stewing steak, cut into 2.5 cm (1 inch) cubes │ 2 garlic cloves, crushed │ 600 ml (1 pint) Beef Stock *(see page 19)* │ 5 star anise │ 1 teaspoon five-spice powder │ 1 cinnamon stick │ 1 teaspoon fennel seeds │ 2 dried kaffir lime leaves │ 1 lemon grass stalk, chopped │ 1 teaspoon black peppercorns │ 2 tablespoons shoyu or tamari sauce │ 400 g (13 oz) carrots, cut into 1 cm (½ inch) slices │ 500 g (1 lb) mooli or turnips, cut into 1 cm (½ inch) slices │ fresh chives, to garnish

ONE Heat the oil in a nonstick sauté pan or wok over a high heat until hot. **TWO** Add the onion, ginger and chillies, stir and cook over a medium heat for about 5–7 minutes. **THREE** Turn up the heat to high, add the beef and fry for about 5–10 minutes until lightly browned, stirring occasionally. **FOUR** Add the garlic, stock, star anise, five-spice powder, cinnamon, fennel seeds, lime leaves, lemon grass, peppercorns and shoyu sauce. Stir and bring the mixture back to the boil then turn down the heat to a simmer. Cover the pan and cook over a low heat for 1½ hours, stirring occasionally. Add the carrots and mooli and continue cooking, covered, for another 45 minutes or until the vegetables have softened. **FIVE** To serve, skim any fat off the surface and garnish with the fresh chives.

Serves 4 as a main dish

NUTRIENT ANALYSIS PER SERVING 1183 kJ – 283 kcal – 30.5 g protein – 17.8 g carbohydrate – 14.6 g sugars – 10.7 g fat – 3.5 g saturates – 3.4 g fibre – 393 mg sodium

HEALTHY TIP Stews and casseroles lend themselves very well to the addition of a variety of root vegetables, such as the carrots and mooli in this recipe. They can be included as a portion of the five-a-day needed for good health.

recipe illustrated on pages 78–79

STEAMED PORK BALLS WITH PLUM RELISH

This is a variation of a Chinese regional Hakka dish from southern China, a very wholesome style of cooking. This dish goes very well with Sticky Rice *(see page 225)* **and Sesame Broccoli** *(see page 169)*.

INGREDIENTS 500 g (1 lb) lean minced pork │ 2 teaspoons shoyu or tamari sauce │ 1 teaspoon sesame oil │ 1 small shallot, finely chopped │ 1 egg, lightly beaten │ 1 tablespoon cornflour │ 1 tablespoon fresh coriander leaves, to garnish

PLUM RELISH 1 star anise, crushed │ ½ teaspoon freshly grated orange rind │ 2 large shallots, chopped │ 1 tablespoon finely grated fresh root ginger │ 2 tablespoons Vegetable Stock *(see page 21)* │ 1 tablespoon plum sauce │ 500 g (1 lb) fresh red plums, stoned and quartered

ONE Mix together the pork, shoyu sauce, sesame oil, shallot, egg and cornflour in a large bowl. Cover and set aside in the refrigerator for about 20 minutes. **TWO** Meanwhile, make the plum relish. Simmer the star anise, orange rind, shallots, ginger, stock, plum sauce and plums over a low heat for about 15 minutes or until the plums are soft. Remove from the heat and set aside to cool. **THREE** Pour about 5 cm (2 inches) of water into a wok, place a metal or wooden rack in the wok and bring the water to the boil. **FOUR** Make the pork balls. Take a tablespoon of the pork mixture and roll it into a ball. Repeat until all the mixture has been used. **FIVE** Put the pork balls in a heatproof bowl and set it on the rack. Cover the wok and steam the pork balls over a high heat for 10–12 minutes or until done. Check the water level from time to time and top up with hot water if necessary. **SIX** Serve the pork balls on a serving dish with the plum sauce and garnish with the coriander leaves.

Serves 4 with 2 other dishes

NUTRIENT ANALYSIS PER SERVING 1124 kJ – 266 kcal – 30.7 g protein – 19.9 g carbohydrate – 12.6 g sugars – 7.8 g fat – 2.4 g saturates – 2.4 g fibre – 194 mg sodium

HEALTHY TIP Plums are a good source of vitamin E, which acts as an antioxidant, helping to protect cells from damage by free radicals and which can help to reduce some of the signs of ageing.

SWEET AND SOUR PORK

This is a Cantonese dish, which is extremely popular in Chinese takeaways and restaurants. However, this recipe uses lean pork rather than the traditional belly pork. Recreate your own takeaway menu by serving this with Vegetable Chop Suey *(see page 194)* and Vegetable Fried Rice *(see page 226)*.

INGREDIENTS 1 egg white, slightly beaten │ 1 teaspoon freshly ground black pepper │ 500 g (1 lb) pork fillet or loin, cut into 1 cm (½ inch) thick slices │ 4 tablespoons cornflour 1 tablespoon rapeseed or olive oil

SWEET AND SOUR SAUCE 3 tablespoons tomato ketchup │ 1 teaspoon white wine vinegar │ 200 g (7 oz) fresh tomatoes, roughly chopped │ 4 tablespoons pineapple juice 2 teaspoons sugar │ 200 ml (7 fl oz) water │ 150 g (5 oz) pineapple pieces │ 150 g (5 oz) green pepper, cored, deseeded and cut into 2.5 cm (1 inch) squares │ 125 g (4 oz) onion, cut into 2.5 cm (1 inch) squares │ juice of 1 lemon

CORNFLOUR PASTE 5 teaspoons cornflour mixed with 5 tablespoons stock or water

ONE Mix the egg white and pepper and rub into the pork slices. Dip each piece of pork into the cornflour, shaking off the excess. **TWO** Heat the oil in a nonstick sauté pan over a high heat until piping hot. **THREE** Put the pork slices into the sauté pan, making sure there is a little space between each one, and fry for 2 minutes on each side. Turn down the heat to medium and stir-fry the pork for another 2 minutes or until done. Transfer to a serving plate and keep warm. **FOUR** Make the sweet and sour sauce. Combine all the ingredients in a small saucepan, bring to the boil and thicken with the cornflour paste. **FIVE** Pour the sauce over the pork and serve.

Serves 4 with 2 other main dishes

NUTRIENT ANALYSIS PER SERVING 1570 kJ – 372 kcal – 26.9 g protein – 44.9 g carbohydrate – 9.7 g sugars – 10.7 g fat – 3.1 g saturates – 1.6 g fibre – 249 mg sodium

HEALTHY TIP Peppers are an excellent source of vitamin C and beta-carotene, both of which act as antioxidants, helping to mop up damaging free radicals. In addition, vitamin C is needed for healthy skin and promoting immune function.

ROAST PORK

Using vinegar in the marinade makes the surface of the pork turn temptingly brown when it's been roasted. The Szechuan peppercorns give the dish an aromatic, citrus flavour without being overpowering. Serve with **Vegetable Fried Rice** *(see page 226)*.

INGREDIENTS 500 g (1 lb) boneless and skinless pork loin │ 2 tablespoons Chinese red wine vinegar or balsamic vinegar │ 1 tablespoon fennel seeds │ ½ tablespoon olive oil │ 1 tablespoon crushed Szechuan peppercorns

ONE Put the pork in a roasting tin with the vinegar, fennel seeds and olive oil. Sprinkle with the peppercorns (don't touch them with your bare hands because they can irritate in the same way as chillies) and set aside to marinate for 30 minutes. **TWO** Cook the pork in a preheated oven, 220°C (425°F), Gas Mark 7, for 40 minutes or until cooked. **THREE** Remove the pork from the oven and leave to cool for 20 minutes in the tin, then slice thinly. Drizzle some gravy from the tin over the meat, if liked.

Serves 4 with 2 other main dishes

NUTRIENT ANALYSIS PER SERVING 754 kJ – 181 kcal – 25.2 g protein – trace carbohydrates – trace sugars – 9.2 g fat – 2.8 g saturates – 0 g fibre – 62 mg sodium

HEALTHY TIP Pork is an excellent source of energy, providing B vitamins and zinc, which are needed to maintain a healthy immune system.

SPARE RIBS

Spare ribs are a popular Chinese dish. This particular recipe has been adapted from one that was a bestseller in my parents-in-law's takeaway. Serve with Steamed Buns *(see page 223)* and Lettuce Wraps *(see page 42)* for an unusual Sunday lunch.

INGREDIENTS 1 kg (2 lb) lean pork spare ribs | 1.2 litres (2 pints) hot Vegetable Stock *(see page 21)* **or a Meat Stock** *(see pages 18, 19 and 20)*

MARINADE 1 teaspoon five spice powder | 2 star anise | 1 tablespoon Szechuan peppercorns | 1 tablespoon black peppercorns | 2 large shallots, chopped | 1 heaped tablespoon hoisin sauce | 1 tablespoon shoyu or tamari sauce | 6 slices fresh root ginger, peeled and crushed | 6 spring onions, chopped | 2 bay leaves, crumbled | 1 orange, cut into wedges

CORNFLOUR PASTE *(optional)* **4 teaspoons cornflour mixed with 4 tablespoons water**

ONE Mix together all the marinade ingredients and rub into the spare ribs. Put them in a shallow dish and marinate in the refrigerator for at least a couple of hours and preferably overnight. **TWO** Line a roasting tin with a large piece of foil. Put the spare ribs and marinade into the tin and pour over the hot stock. Cook for 1 hour in a preheated oven, 240°C (475°F), Gas Mark 9, then turn the ribs over. **THREE** Reduce the heat to 180°C (350°F), Gas Mark 4 and cook for a further 45 minutes or until the ribs are browned and soft. **FOUR** Remove the ribs with a slotted spoon and place on a serving plate. Pour the remaining sauce from the bottom of the roasting tin into a small saucepan and thicken with some cornflour paste, if you like, stirring until the sauce has thickened and turned transparent.

Serves 4

NUTRIENT ANALYSIS PER SERVING 1993 kJ – 275 kcal – 62.7 g protein – 10.9 g carbohydrate – 6.7 g sugars – 20.5 g fat – 7.2 g saturates – 1.5 g fibre – 297 mg sodium

HEALTHY TIP Spare ribs can be high in fat, particularly if they are deep-fried. Removing any excess visible fat before and after cooking will help reduce the fat content.

recipe illustrated on pages 88–89

PORK SATAY

This popular South-east Asian dish is ideal for barbecues. The satay sauce can be prepared beforehand, and you can use other meats, such as chicken, beef or lamb, or even prawns instead of the pork.

INGREDIENTS 1 teaspoon ground turmeric | 1 teaspoon ground coriander | 1 teaspoon ground cumin | 1 tablespoon lime juice | 1 tablespoon shoyu or tamari sauce | 1 teaspoon sesame oil | 500 g (1 lb) pork fillet, cut into 5 mm (¼ inch) x 1 cm (½ inch) pieces

SATAY SAUCE 250 ml (8 fl oz) light coconut milk | 50 g (2 oz) reduced-fat peanut butter | 2 teaspoons red curry paste | ½ teaspoon lime juice

ONE Soak some wooden satay sticks in water for 15–20 minutes. **TWO** Mix the turmeric, coriander, cumin, lime juice and shoyu sauce and rub into the pork fillet. Cover and chill for at least 1 hour. **THREE** Mix all the sauce ingredients in a small saucepan and simmer for 20 minutes, stirring occasionally to prevent the sauce sticking to the pan. Transfer to a small bowl and leave to cool. **FOUR** Thread 3–4 pork cubes on to each satay stick. **FIVE** Place the satay sticks on a roasting rack under a preheated very hot grill and cook for 10–12 minutes or until done, turning them frequently to prevent burning.

Serves 4 as a light meal

NUTRIENT ANALYSIS PER SERVING, INCLUDING THE SAUCE 915 kJ – 278 kcal – 28.1 g protein – 6.4 g carbohydrate – 4.5 g sugars – 15.4 g fat – 6.2 g saturates – 1.5 g fibre – 192 mg sodium

POULTRY

CHICKEN WITH LEMON GRASS AND ASPARAGUS

This dish has a Thai influence, with lots of lemon grass, ginger and basil leaves. The addition of vine-ripened tomatoes moistens the dish and lends a taste of the Mediterranean. Serve with Prawn and Grapefruit Salad *(see page 48)* as a starter.

INGREDIENTS 1 tablespoon rapeseed or olive oil │ 2 garlic cloves, crushed │ 2 tablespoons finely chopped lemon grass │ 2 teaspoons finely chopped fresh root ginger │ 1 onion, sliced │ 500 g (1 lb) chicken breast, cut into strips │ 300 g (10 oz) vine-ripened tomatoes, chopped │ 350 g (12 oz) asparagus spears, halved length- and widthways │ 1 tablespoon shoyu or tamari sauce │ ½ teaspoon ground black pepper │ handful of Thai basil leaves, to garnish

ONE Heat the oil in a nonstick sauté pan over a high heat until hot, swirling it around the pan. **TWO** Toss in the garlic, lemon grass, ginger and onion and stir-fry for about 5 minutes. **THREE** Add the chicken and stir-fry for about 5–7 minutes until the chicken is browned and cooked. **FOUR** Add the tomatoes, asparagus, shoyu sauce and pepper and stir-fry for about 2–3 minutes to warm through. Garnish with the Thai basil leaves.

Serves 4

NUTRIENT ANALYSIS PER SERVING 825 kJ – 196 kcal – 30.9 g protein – 7.7 g carbohydrate – 6.2 g sugars – 4.8 g fat – 0.9 g saturates – 2.9 g fibre – 202 mg sodium

HEALTHY TIP Asparagus is best eaten on the day it's bought, since it loses its freshness rapidly when stored. In folk medicine, it is used as a tonic to treat various ills, including rheumatism and toothache.

recipe illustrated on pages 98–99

CHANDOORI CHICKEN

This is my Chinese version of tandoori chicken, flavoured with an oriental mix of spices and roasted in the oven. It can also be cooked on a barbecue. This dish is best served as finger food with cucumber sticks and roasted sweet potato slices and a Tofu and Mirin Dressing *(see page 25)* or a Chilli Dipping Sauce *(see page 26)*.

INGREDIENTS 4 x 100 g (3½ oz) boneless, skinless chicken thighs │ 1 lime, cut into wedges

MARINADE 1 star anise │ 1 teaspoon Szechuan peppercorns │ 1 teaspoon black peppercorns │ 1 lemon grass stalk, finely chopped │ 2 garlic cloves, crushed │ 1 teaspoon finely chopped fresh root ginger │ 1 tablespoon shoyu or tamari sauce │ 1 teaspoon sesame oil │ 1 teaspoon five spice powder

ONE Make the marinade. Coarsely pound the star anise, Szechuan and black peppercorns, lemon grass, garlic and ginger to a paste in a mortar. Mix in the shoyu sauce, sesame oil and five spice powder until well blended. **TWO** Put the chicken thighs in a bowl and rub with the marinade. Cover and chill for at least 1 hour. **THREE** Transfer the chicken thighs to a rack and cook in a preheated oven, 240°C (475°F), Gas Mark 9, for 20 minutes or until done.

Serves 4 with a side dish as a light lunch or supper

NUTRIENT ANALYSIS PER SERVING 504 kJ – 120 kcal – 21.5 g protein – 0.7 g carbohydrate – 0.1 g sugars – 3.7 g fat – 0.9 g saturates – 0.1 g fibre – 21 mg sodium

HEALTHY TIP Chicken is naturally low in fat. Grilling instead of frying in oil is a great way of serving a delicious light meal for those who are watching their waistlines.

recipe illustrated on pages 102–103

DUCK AND PINEAPPLE

INGREDIENTS 2 x 100 g (3½ oz) Gressingham duck breasts, skin removed │ ½ teaspoon sesame oil │ ½ teaspoon freshly ground black pepper │ 250 g (8 oz) pineapple chunks, canned in juice │ 2 slices fresh root ginger │ 1 tablespoon shoyu or tamari sauce

CORNFLOUR PASTE 1 teaspoon cornflour mixed with 2 tablespoons water

ONE Rub the duck breasts with the sesame oil and black pepper and set aside. **TWO** Heat a griddle pan over a high heat until piping hot. Add the duck breasts and cook for 2–3 minutes on each side for medium done. Remove and blot any excess oil on kitchen paper. **THREE** To make the sauce, pour the pineapple chunks and their juice into a pan, add the ginger slices and cook over a medium heat for about 3–4 minutes. Stir in the shoyu sauce and bring the mixture to the boil. Slowly stir in the cornflour paste, a little at a time, to thicken the sauce. **FOUR** To serve, pour the sauce on to a serving plate. Slice the duck breasts and arrange them on the sauce. This dish goes very well with a mixture of jasmine and wild rice.

Serves 4 with 2 other dishes

NUTRIENT ANALYSIS PER SERVING 1007 kJ – 240 kcal – 23.9 g protein – 14.3 g carbohydrate – 6.9 g sugars – 10.1 g fat – 3.1 g saturates – 0.3 g fibre – 219 mg sodium

HEALTHY TIP A typical 100 g (3½ oz) serving of duck meat and skin will supply 29 g (about 1¼ oz) fat, while the fat content of duck meat only is 10 g (⅓ oz). Duck is a good source of the B vitamins thiamin and riboflavin and contains more iron than chicken.

CHICKEN CHOP SUEY

INGREDIENTS ½ teaspoon rapeseed or olive oil │ 1 teaspoon sesame oil │ 1 large shallot, finely chopped │ 1 garlic clove, crushed │ 200 g (7 oz) chicken breast, sliced into strips │ 350 g (11½ oz) fresh beansprouts │ 50 g (2 oz) canned sliced bamboo shoots, drained │ 100 g (3½ oz) canned tomatoes, drained and crushed │ 2 teaspoons shoyu or tamari sauce │ 2 spring onions, chopped lengthways

ONE Heat the rapeseed and sesame oils in a nonstick sauté pan until hot. Add the shallot and garlic and stir-fry over medium heat for 1 minute until the shallot begins to turn transparent. **TWO** Turn up the heat to high, add the chicken strips and stir-fry for about 5 minutes or until cooked. **THREE** Quickly add the beansprouts, bamboo shoots, crushed tomatoes, shoyu sauce and spring onions and stir-fry for about 30 seconds until the beansprouts have started to wilt slightly. **FOUR** Serve immediately.

Serves 4 with 2 other main dishes

NUTRIENT ANALYSIS PER SERVING 481 kJ – 114 kcal – 15.5 g protein – 6.0 g carbohydrate – 3.7 g sugars – 3.4 g fat · 0.6 g saturates – 2.0 g fibre – 129 mg sodium

HEALTHY TIP Sprouted mung or other beans are great sources of vitamin C. A portion of beansprouts will provide three-quarters of an adult's daily requirement. Sprouting increases the content of B vitamins in beans and also makes the protein easier to digest.

SAUTEED CHICKEN LIVERS

INGREDIENTS ½ tablespoon rapeseed or olive oil │ 1 garlic clove, crushed │ 1 slice fresh root ginger, peeled and roughly chopped │ 2 shallots, sliced │ 12 chicken livers, weighing about 250 g (8 oz), trimmed │ 250 ml (8 fl oz) Chicken Stock *(see page 18)* │ 1 teaspoon balsamic vinegar │ 1 tablespoon rice wine or dry sherry │ 2 teaspoons shoyu or tamari sauce

ONE Heat the oil in a nonstick sauté pan or wok over a high heat until piping hot. Swirl the oil around the pan, add the garlic, ginger and shallots and stir-fry for a few seconds. **TWO** Add the chicken livers and cook for 1 minute on each side. **THREE** Add the stock, vinegar, rice wine and shoyu sauce and bring to the boil, then simmer for a couple of minutes until the stock has reduced and thickened.

Serves 4 with 2 other main dishes

NUTRIENT ANALYSIS PER SERVING 498 kJ – 119 kcal – 17.4 g protein – 1.0 g carbohydrate – 0.5 g sugars – 5.0 g fat – 1.1 g saturates – 0.2 g fibre – 158 mg sodium

KUNG PO CHICKEN

INGREDIENTS 1 tablespoon rapeseed or olive oil | 2–3 red chillies, deseeded and sliced | 2 garlic cloves, finely chopped | 400 g (13 oz) chicken breast, cut into 1 cm (½ inch) cubes | 1 teaspoon chilli bean sauce | 50 g (2 oz) canned sliced bamboo shoots, drained | 50 g (2 oz) canned water chestnuts, drained | 1 tablespoon Chinese rice wine or dry sherry | 100 ml (3½ fl oz) Chicken Stock (see page 17) or water | 50 g (2 oz) roasted unsalted peanuts | 2 spring onions, cut into 1 cm (½ inch) lengths

CORNFLOUR PASTE 1 teaspoon cornflour mixed with 1 tablespoon water

ONE Heat the oil in a nonstick sauté pan over high heat, add the chillies and garlic and stir-fry for a few seconds. **TWO** Add the chicken and chilli bean sauce and stir-fry for a couple of minutes, then add the bamboo shoots, water chestnuts, rice wine and stock and bring to the boil. Slowly add the cornflour paste, stirring until the sauce has thickened and turned transparent. **THREE** Mix in the peanuts and spring onions just before serving.

Serves 4 with 2 other main dishes

NUTRIENT ANALYSIS PER SERVING 941 kJ – 224 kcal – 27.8 g protein – 5.8 g carbohydrate – 2.0 g sugars – 9.7 g fat – 1.6 g saturates – 1.1 g fibre – 85 mg sodium

CHICKEN WITH LYCHEES AND MELON

This is an adaptation of the winning recipe created by Mrs Jacky Williams in the Chinese Healthy Cooking Competition, which was jointly sponsored by the British Heart Foundation and the Chinese National Healthy Living Centre in London. Serve this dish with Sticky Rice *(see page 225)* and Stir-fried Tofu with Assorted Vegetables *(see page 176)*.

INGREDIENTS ½ teaspoon sesame oil │ 2 teaspoons cornflour │ 2 teaspoons shoyu or tamari sauce │ 400 g (13 oz) chicken breast, cut into strips │ 1 medium honeydew melon │ 1 tablespoon rapeseed or olive oil │ 1 garlic clove, crushed │ 2 slices fresh root ginger │ 50 ml (2 fl oz) Chicken Stock *(see page 18)* │ 1 tablespoon honey │ 12–15 fresh lychees, peeled and stoned │ 2 spring onions, sliced

ONE Mix the sesame oil, cornflour and shoyu sauce and rub into the chicken. Set aside for 10 minutes. **TWO** Cut the top off the melon and remove the seeds with a spoon. Scoop out the flesh with a teaspoon or a melon baller and set aside. You should now be left with a melon bowl. **THREE** Heat the oil in a nonstick sauté pan over a high heat. Add the garlic and ginger and stir-fry for about 1 minute. **FOUR** Add the marinated chicken and stir-fry for about 3–4 minutes until lightly browned. Pour in the chicken stock and bring to the boil. **FIVE** Drizzle the honey over the chicken, then stir in the lychees and melon balls to warm through. **SIX** Sprinkle with the spring onions then transfer the dish to the melon bowl to serve.

Serves 4

NUTRIENT ANALYSIS PER SERVING 915 kJ – 216 kcal – 25.5 g protein – 19.9 g carbohydrate – 17.1 g sugars – 4.5 g fat – 0.8 g saturates – 1.1 g fibre – 186 mg sodium

HEALTHY TIP Melons are a good source of vitamin C. They also have a high water content which makes them efficient thirst-quenchers. Orange- and pink-fleshed varieties, such as canteloupe melons, are also rich in beta-carotene.

CHICKEN AND CASHEW NUTS WITH VEGETABLES

This dish is a firm favourite on the Chinese takeaway menu. This low-fat version needs no oil as the chicken breast meat is simmered in stock.

INGREDIENTS 250 ml (8 fl oz) Chicken Stock *(see page 18)* | 400 g (13 oz) chicken breast, cubed | 2 tablespoons yellow bean sauce | 200 g (7 oz) carrots, sliced | 200 g (7 oz) bamboo shoots, sliced | 200 g (7 oz) cashew nuts, toasted | 1 spring onion, shredded

CORNFLOUR PASTE 1 teaspoon cornflour mixed with 2 tablespoons water or stock

ONE Heat the chicken stock in a saucepan. Add the chicken meat and bring the liquid back to the boil, stirring. Lower the heat and cook for 5 minutes. Remove the chicken with a slotted spoon and set aside. **TWO** Add the yellow bean sauce and cook for a couple of minutes. Add the carrots and bamboo shoots and cook for another couple of minutes. **THREE** Return the chicken to the pan, bring the sauce back to the boil and thicken with cornflour paste. **FOUR** Stir in the cashew nuts and spring onion just before serving.

Serves 4 with 2 other main dishes

NUTRIENT ANALYSIS PER SERVING 1549 kJ – 371 kcal – 33.3 g protein – 15.2 g carbohydrate – 7.6 g sugars – 20.0 g fat – 4.1 g saturates – 3.3 g fibre – 268 mg sodium

LEMON CHICKEN

In this classic Cantonese dish the chicken is often deep-fried and served with a fairly thick lemon sauce. The chicken in this recipe is pan-fried and contains almost no sauce, only subtle overtones of fresh lemon juice and the lemon oil, which is released from the lemon rind as it cooks. Serve it with Shredded Beef with Carrots and Chilli *(see page 69)* and stir-fried vegetables to celebrate a marriage of Cantonese and Szechuan cuisine.

INGREDIENTS 1 egg, lightly beaten | 2 garlic cloves, sliced | 2 small pieces of unwaxed lemon rind | 500 g (1 lb) skinless chicken breast, cut into 5 mm (¼ inch) slices | 2 tablespoons cornflour | 1 tablespoon rapeseed or olive oil | juice of 1 lemon | 1 spring onion, chopped diagonally into 1.5 cm (¾ inch) lengths | lemon slices, to garnish

ONE Combine the egg, garlic and lemon rind and marinate the chicken for 10–15 minutes. **TWO** Remove the lemon rind and add the cornflour to the marinated chicken. Mix thoroughly to distribute the cornflour evenly among the chicken slices. **THREE** Heat the oil in a nonstick sauté pan over a high heat. Add the chicken slices, making sure you leave a little space between them. **FOUR** Fry the chicken slices for 2 minutes on each side. **FIVE** Reduce the heat to medium and stir-fry for 1 more minute or until the chicken is browned and cooked. Turn up the heat and pour in the lemon juice. Add the spring onion, garnish with lemon slices and serve immediately.

Serves 4 with 2 other main dishes

NUTRIENT ANALYSIS PER SERVING 987 kJ – 234 kcal – 32 g protein – 14.0 g carbohydrate – 0.1 g sugars – 5.8 g fat – 1.2 g saturates – 0.1 g fibre – 103 mg sodium

HEALTHY TIP Lemon juice is a great alternative seasoning to salt or soy sauce. Lemons are an excellent source of vitamin C, which can help to fight infection by maintaining a healthy immune system.

recipe illustrated on pages 116–117

SESAME CHICKEN WITH CUCUMBER

This Szechuan dish is sometimes known as pang-pang or bon-bon chicken and usually contains a fiery mix of chilli oil and chilli flakes. The heat in this recipe comes from a subtle addition of mustard, which gives the chicken a slight tang without being too overpowering. Serve with a hearty bowl of Hot and Sour Soup *(see page 60)* and Steamed Buns *(see page 223)*.

INGREDIENTS 400 g (13 oz) cooked chicken breast, shredded │ 375 g (12 oz) cucumber, sliced

DRESSING 4 spring onions, sliced │ 4 teaspoons sesame paste │ 1 tablespoon white wine vinegar │ 2 teaspoons English mustard

ONE Mix all the ingredients for the dressing in a large bowl. Add the shredded chicken and toss to mix thoroughly. **TWO** To serve, put the cucumber slices on a large serving plate and top with the dressed chicken.

Serves 4 as a light meal

NUTRIENT ANALYSIS PER SERVING 1117 kJ – 268 kcal – 33.5 g protein – 2.2 g carbohydrate – 2.0 g sugars – 13.8 g fat – 2.8 g saturates – 1.9 g fibre – 195 mg sodium

HEALTHY TIP Cucumber has a high water content and is very low in calories, which makes it a great friend for anyone who is on a diet.

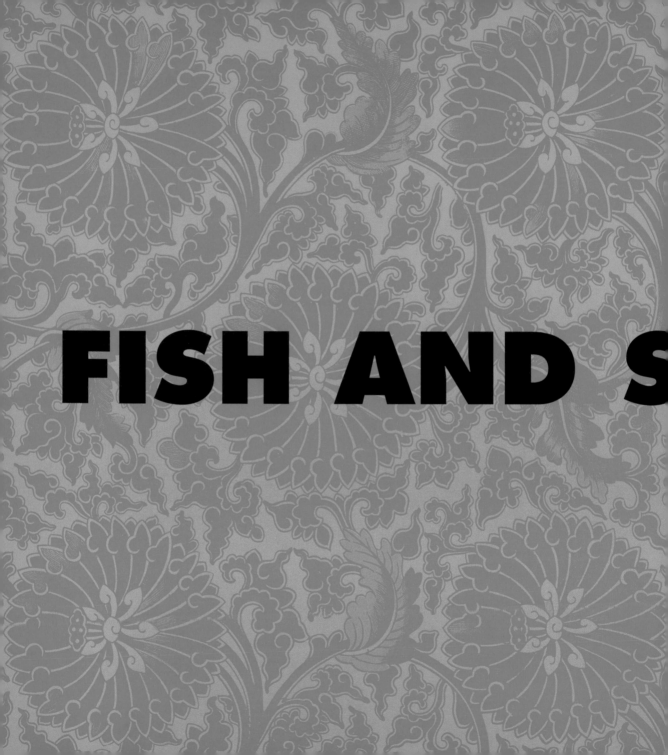

FISH AND S

SESAME SALMON WITH SHREDDED VEGETABLES

INGREDIENTS 500 g (1 lb) thick salmon fillets, skinned | 1 tablespoon gomasio salt | juice of ½ lime | 1 tablespoon raw sesame seeds | 1 large leek, shredded | 2 large carrots, shredded | 125 g (4 oz) mangetout, shredded

ONE Put the salmon fillets in a foil-lined roasting tin and sprinkle with gomasio salt, lime juice and sesame seeds. Cook in a preheated oven, 240°C (425°F), Gas Mark 9, for 15–20 minutes or until the salmon is just cooked and the sesame seeds are toasted and browned. **TWO** Meanwhile, toss together the leek, carrots and mangetout and arrange on a serving dish. **THREE** To serve, place the salmon on the bed of vegetables and pour over the juices from the roasting tin.

Serves 4 with 2 other main dishes

NUTRIENT ANALYSIS PER SERVING 1126 kJ – 270 kcal – 24.8 g protein – 7.7 g carbohydrate – 6.8 g sugars – 15.8 g fat – 2.7 g saturates – 3.0 g fibre – 111 mg sodium

HEALTHY TIP Oily fish contain omega-3 fatty acids, which are believed to help protect against heart and circulation problems.

KING PRAWNS WITH GINGER AND SPRING ONIONS

Spring onions and ginger are classic accompaniments to fish and shellfish dishes in Cantonese cuisine. This recipe uses both ingredients to create a quick and easy weekday supper dish. This dish goes really well with Sweet and Sour Pork *(see page 82)*.

INGREDIENTS ½ tablespoon rapeseed oil │ 2 garlic cloves, crushed │ 3–4 slices fresh root ginger, peeled and shredded │ 400 g (13 oz) large, raw prawns (with shells), deveined │ 2 teaspoons shoyu or tamari sauce │ 2 teaspoons dry sherry │ ½ teaspoon sesame oil │ ½ teaspoon freshly ground black pepper │ 4 tablespoons Vegetable Stock *(see page 21)* │ 2 spring onions, shredded into 1.5 cm (¾ inch) lengths, to serve

CORNFLOUR PASTE 1 teaspoon cornflour mixed with 1 tablespoon water

ONE Heat the oil in a nonstick sauté pan and stir-fry the garlic and ginger for a few seconds. **TWO** Add the prawns and stir-fry for about 1 minute until almost cooked. **THREE** Season with shoyu sauce, sherry, sesame oil and pepper and add the stock. Stir in the cornflour paste to thicken the sauce. **FOUR** Sprinkle with the spring onions and serve immediately.

Serves 4 with 2 other dishes

NUTRIENT ANALYSIS PER SERVING 423 kJ – 101 kcal – 19.0 g protein – 0.9 g carbohydrate – 0.3 g sugars – 2.7 g fat – 0.4 g saturates – 0.2 g fibre – 274 mg sodium

HEALTHY TIP Ginger is a favourite spice in oriental cooking. In traditional Chinese medicine, it is thought to improve blood circulation and is also recommended as a cure for travel sickness and morning sickness.

recipe illustrated on pages 128–129

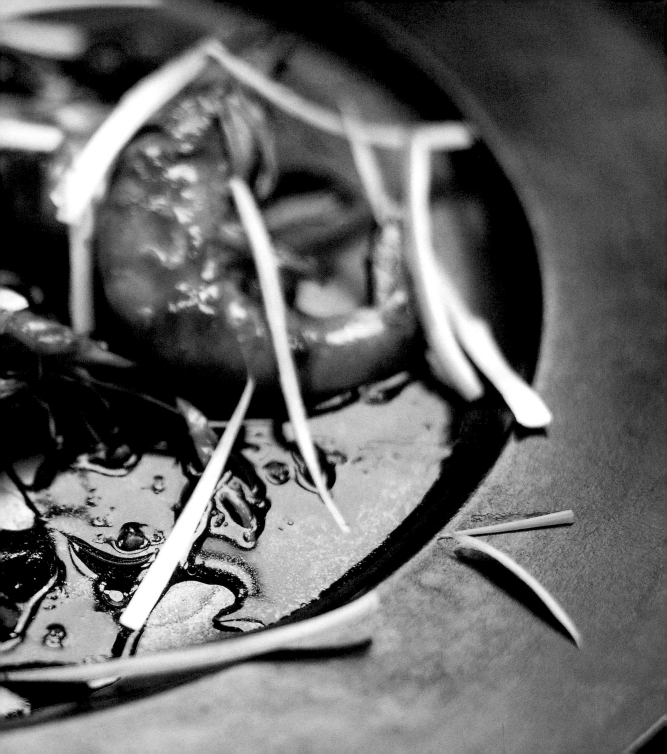

GARLIC STEAMED PRAWNS

This recipe is ideal for cooking larger prawns. Since you need to dig in with your fingers to enjoy this dish, you might as well go the whole hog and serve it with another dish that requires hands-on treatment, so try it with **Mussels with Basil and Black Bean Sauce** *(see page 146)* for the ultimate seafood experience.

INGREDIENTS 400 g (13 oz) large, raw prawns (with shells), heads removed │ 1 teaspoon olive oil │ 4–5 garlic cloves, crushed │ 1 teaspoon shoyu or tamari sauce │ 1 teaspoon Chinese rice wine or dry sherry │ ½ teaspoon ground black pepper │ 1 tablespoon chopped fresh coriander, to garnish

ONE Using a pair of scissors, cut the prawns down the back from the head to the tail end, to form a butterfly shape. Remove and discard the vein and arrange the prawns in a circle on a heatproof dish. **TWO** Pour about 5 cm (2 inches) water into a wok, place a metal or wooden rack in the wok and bring the water to the boil. **THREE** Mix the olive oil with the garlic, shoyu sauce, rice wine and black pepper and spoon over the prawns. **FOUR** Put the heatproof dish on the rack, cover and steam over a high heat for 3 minutes or until the prawns have turned pink and are cooked. **FIVE** To serve, carefully remove the dish from the wok and scatter the coriander leaves over the top.

Serves 4 with 2 other dishes

NUTRIENT ANALYSIS PER SERVING 363 kJ – 86 kcal – 17.8 g protein – 0.4 g carbohydrate – 0.1 g sugars – 1.4 g fat – 0.2 g saturates – 0.1 g fibre – 191 mg sodium

HEALTHY TIP Some scientific studies have shown that daily doses of garlic may help to lower blood pressure and cholesterol. Garlic is also thought to have antiviral and antibacterial properties.

OYSTERS WITH BLACK BEAN SAUCE

Oysters are often deep-fried in batter, which cooks them quickly, sealing in the natural juices. Although deep-fried oysters are delicious, they can also be high in fat. This low-fat version is pan-fried, which also ensures rapid cooking. In addition, their natural flavour is enhanced by garlic, spring onions and black bean sauce. Fish and shellfish meal combinations are common in Chinese restaurants. Try combining these oysters with **Poached Scallops with Wasabi Dressing** (see page 152) **and Monkfish Stir-fried with Celery** (see page 154) .

INGREDIENTS 1 tablespoon rapeseed or olive oil │ 4 thin slices fresh root ginger │ 2 garlic cloves, crushed │ 2 tablespoons black bean sauce │ 24 oysters, shucked │ 4 spring onions, diagonally sliced │ 1 tablespoon Chinese rice wine or dry sherry │ ½ teaspoon sesame oil

ONE Heat the oil in a nonstick sauté pan or wok over a high heat. Add the ginger and garlic and stir-fry for a few seconds until lightly browned. **TWO** Stir in the black bean sauce, then add the oysters. Cover the pan with a lid and cook the oysters over a high heat for 30 seconds. **THREE** Remove the lid and add the spring onions, rice wine and sesame oil. Stir and serve immediately.

Serves 4

NUTRIENT ANALYSIS PER SERVING 352 kJ – 84 kcal – 7.4 g protein – 3.5 g carbohydrate – 1.3 g sugars – 4.1 g fat – 0.6 g saturates – 0.5 g fibre – 496 mg sodium

HEALTHY TIP Oysters have long been used as aphrodisiacs. Although the scientific basis for this is unclear, they are rich in the mineral zinc, which is needed for sperm production and a healthy libido.

SWEET AND SOUR PRAWNS

INGREDIENTS 1 teaspoon olive oil | 1 garlic clove, chopped | 1 teaspoon chopped fresh root ginger | 150 ml (¼ pint) **Vegetable Stock** *(see page 21)* | 150 g (5 oz) plum tomatoes, chopped | 1 tablespoon tomato ketchup | 1 tablespoon white wine vinegar | 1 tablespoon light muscavado sugar | 500 g (1 lb) fresh or frozen raw prawns, peeled and deveined | 150 g (5 oz) canned pineapple chunks, drained | 150 g (5 oz) green pepper, chopped | 1 spring onion, chopped lengthways

CORNFLOUR PASTE 1 teaspoon cornflour mixed with 6 tablespoons water or stock

ONE Heat the oil in a nonstick pan, add the garlic and ginger and fry for about 20 seconds.

TWO Add the stock, tomatoes, tomato ketchup, vinegar and sugar and bring to the boil.

THREE Add the prawns, cook for about 1 minute, then add the pineapple chunks and green pepper. Bring the mixture back to the boil and thicken with the cornflour paste.

FOUR Sprinkle with spring onion and serve immediately with Boiled Rice *(see page 224)* or thin egg noodles to soak up the lovely sweet and sour sauce.

Serves 4 with 2 other main dishes

NUTRIENT ANALYSIS PER SERVING 742 kJ – 175 kcal – 24.6 g protein – 15.4 g carbohydrate – 11.6 g sugars – 2.1 g fat – 0.4 g saturates – 1.3 g fibre – 1104 mg sodium

MIXED SEAFOOD WITH BEANTHREAD NOODLES

Beanthread or cellophane noodles are lighter than rice vermicelli and have a firmer, more robust texture. They can absorb plenty of liquids and flavours.

INGREDIENTS 1 tablespoon rapeseed or olive oil │ 2 garlic cloves, chopped │ 2 slices fresh ginger, chopped │ 1 tablespoon chilli bean sauce │ 2 teaspoons shoyu or tamari sauce │ 1 teaspoon freshly ground white pepper │ 2 litres (3½ pints) Fish Stock *(see page 22)* or Vegetable Stock *(see page 21)* │ 225 g (7½ oz) Chinese leaves, cut into 2.5 cm (1 inch) strips │ 175 g (6 oz) dried beanthread or cellophane noodles │ 125 g (4 oz) each raw prawns, scallops and squid │ 1 tablespoon fresh coriander leaves, to garnish

ONE Heat the oil in a nonstick sauté pan or wok over a high heat until hot. Add the garlic and ginger and stir-fry for a few seconds until fragrant. **TWO** Stir in the chilli bean sauce, shoyu sauce, pepper and stock and bring to the boil. Add the Chinese leaves, turn down the heat to medium and simmer for 10 minutes. **THREE** Add the beanthread noodles, cover the pan and simmer for another 5 minutes. **FOUR** Add the mixed seafood, stir and bring back to the boil and simmer for 1 more minute. Serve in a deep dish and garnish with coriander leaves.

Serves 4–6 with 2 other dishes

NUTRIENT ANALYSIS PER SERVING 1116 kJ – 267 kcal – 21.3 g protein – 36.7 g carbohydrate – 1.9 g sugars – 3.7 g fat – 0.5 g saturates – 0.8 g fibre – 315 mg sodium

HEALTHY TIP Beanthread noodles are made from mung beans and are often eaten as vegetables rather than as carbohydrate foods as rice or buckwheat noodles are.

recipe illustrated on pages 138–139

CRAB MEAT WITH ASPARAGUS

Crab can be overpowered by a sauce that is too rich or too spicy, but the light sauce in this recipe goes really well with it. The combination of crab and tender asparagus brings a mixture of sweetness and crunchiness to each mouthful. This dish goes well with Fu Yung with Vegetables *(see page 188)*.

INGREDIENTS 1 tablespoon rapeseed or olive oil │ 1 slice fresh root ginger │ 1 garlic clove, crushed │ 1 tablespoon Chinese rice wine or dry sherry │ 100 ml (3½ fl oz) Vegetable Stock *(see page 21)* │ 625 g (1¼ lb) asparagus, trimmed, cut into pieces 3 cm (1¼ inches) long │ 250 g (8 oz) cooked crab meat │ 1 teaspoon shoyu or tamari sauce │ 2 spring onions, thinly sliced, to serve

CORNFLOUR PASTE 1 teaspoon cornflour mixed with 5 tablespoons Vegetable Stock *(see pagc 21)* **or water**

ONE Heat the oil in a nonstick sauté pan over a high heat. Add the ginger and garlic and stir-fry for a few seconds. **TWO** Pour in the wine and stock and bring to the boil. Add the asparagus, cook over a high heat for 2–3 minutes, then remove with a slotted spoon to a serving plate. **THREE** Add the crab meat and shoyu sauce. Bring the mixture back to the boil and slowly add the cornflour paste, stirring continuously until the sauce has thickened. **FOUR** To serve, spoon the crab sauce over the asparagus and sprinkle with the spring onions.

Serves 4 with 2 other main dishes

NUTRIENT ANALYSIS PER SERVING 642 kJ – 154 kcal – 16.8 g protein – 5.8 g carbohydrate – 3.0 g sugars – 7.1 g fat – 1.0 g saturates – 2.7 g fibre – 308 mg sodium

HEALTHY TIP Asparagus is a rich source of the B vitamin folate. A 100 g (3½ oz) serving provides three-quarters of an adult's daily requirement of folate, which is needed for making healthy blood. It is also valuable for pregnant women to help reduce the risk of having babies with neural tube defects.

SQUID STIR-FRIED WITH MANGETOUT

Fresh squid has an intense sweet flavour, which is further enhanced by combining it with fresh, crispy mangetout in this dish. Seasonings are kept light, with the Szechuan peppercorns adding a subtle but clean citrus flavour. This dish goes well with stir-fried chicken dishes and stir-fried green beans.

INGREDIENTS 250 g (8 oz) squid, cleaned | 1 tablespoon rapeseed or olive oil | 1 green chilli, chopped | 2 teaspoons Szechuan peppercorns, crushed | 2 garlic cloves, crushed | 1 small onion, chopped | 250 g (8 oz) mangetout | 2 teaspoons shoyu or tamari sauce | 1 tablespoon Chinese rice wine or dry sherry

ONE Cut the squid into slices and score with a criss-cross pattern (this makes them curl up when they are cooked, and the grooves help to trap the sauce). **TWO** Heat the oil in a nonstick sauté pan over a high heat until hot. Add the chilli, peppercorns, garlic and onion and stir-fry over a medium heat for about 3–4 minutes. **THREE** Turn the heat to high, add the squid slices and stir-fry quickly for 1 minute then remove them from the pan. **FOUR** Toss in the mangetout and stir-fry for 1 minute then return the squid to the pan. Stir to mix, add the shoyu and rice wine and stir-fry for a few seconds then serve immediately.

Serves 2 with another main dish

NUTRIENT ANALYSIS PER SERVING 450 kJ – 107 kcal – 12.3 g protein – 4.8 g carbohydrate – 3.0 g sugars – 4.0 g fat – 0.6 g saturates – 1.7 g fibre – 154 mg sodium

HEALTHY TIP Squid is a good source of the mineral selenium. Selenium is needed for healthy hair and skin and there is also some scientific evidence that it helps to protect against prostate cancer.

recipe illustrated on pages 144–145

MUSSELS WITH BASIL AND BLACK BEAN SAUCE

An oriental version of moules marinière, this fragrant and spicy dish is great on a cold, wintry night. Serve as a light lunch with Noodles with Aromatic Prawns *(see page 218)*.

INGREDIENTS 1 tablespoon rapeseed or olive oil │ ½ teaspoon freshly ground black pepper │ 2 red chillies, deseeded and sliced │ 2 garlic cloves, crushed │ 1 kg (2 lb) mussels, scrubbed and debearded │ 60 ml (2 fl oz) Fish Stock *(see page 22)* │ 1 tablespoon black bean sauce │ 1 tablespoon Chinese rice wine or dry sherry │ large handful of fresh coriander leaves │ large handful of fresh Thai basil leaves

ONE Heat the oil in a wok over a high heat until hot. Add the pepper, chillies and garlic and stir-fry for about 30 seconds until fragrant. **TWO** Add the mussels to the wok and stir to mix, then add the stock, black bean sauce and rice wine or sherry. Cover the pan and cook for about 2 minutes until the mussels have opened. **THREE** Toss in the coriander and basil leaves then transfer the mussels to a large serving dish, discarding any that have not opened. Serve immediately.

Serves 4–6 with 2 other main dishes

NUTRIENT ANALYSIS PER SERVING 927 kJ – 221 kcal – 30.8 g protein – 7.2 g carbohydrate – 0.5 g sugars – 7.4 g fat – 1.4 g saturates – 0.1 g fibre – 821 mg sodium

HEALTHY TIP Mussels are a rich source of the minerals iodine and iron. Shellfish are the best source of iodine, which is needed to make thyroid hormones that control the rate at which the body uses energy.

recipe illustrated on pages 148–149

SEA BASS WITH SPRING ONION AND GINGER DRESSING

Traditionally, Chinese people prefer whole fish to fillets. This recipe is simpler to eat and there's no need to worry about bones. Other fish that can be used as a variation include turbot and halibut. Chinese people often combine delicate fish dishes with other equally subtle flavours and stir-fried vegetables for a low-fat meal.

INGREDIENTS 4 x 175 g (6 oz) sea bass fillets | 1 tablespoon rapeseed oil | 4 spring onions, finely shredded | 4 slices fresh ginger, peeled and finely shredded | 2 tablespoons Fish Stock *(see page 22)* | 2 teaspoons shoyu or tamari sauce | 2 teaspoons Chinese rice wine or dry sherry

ONE Half-fill a wok with water, place a metal or wooden rack in the wok and bring the water to the boil over a high heat. **TWO** Meanwhile, put the sea bass fillets on a shallow plate and put it on the rack as soon as the water has boiled. Cover the wok and steam the sea bass over a high heat for 7–8 minutes. **THREE** To prepare the sauce, heat the oil in a small saucepan over a medium heat. Add the spring onions and ginger and stir-fry for a few seconds, then add the stock, shoyu sauce and rice wine. Stir and cook for a few more seconds then remove the pan from the heat. **FOUR** Remove the steamed fillets from the wok and pour the warm dressing over them. Serve immediately.

Serves 4 with 2 other main dishes

NUTRIENT ANALYSIS PER SERVING 874 kJ – 208 kcal – 34.2 g protein – 0.9 g carbohydrate – 0.4 g sugars – 7.2 g fat – 0.9 g saturates – 0.2 g fibre – 205 mg sodium

HEALTHY TIP Steaming is a convenient and delicious way of cooking food without adding oil. Foods are cooked gently and evenly because the heat doesn't rise above boiling point.

POACHED SCALLOPS WITH WASABI DRESSING

This recipe is ideal for king scallops; poaching them in stock ensures gentle cooking and preserves their sweet succulent flavour. Wasabi paste is a Japanese mustard, so pungent that it's been nicknamed 'namida' or 'tears' in traditional sushi bars. So, be warned.

INGREDIENTS 1.2 litres (2 pints) Fish Stock *(see page 22)* | 16 king scallops, shelled

DRESSING 1 teaspoon wasabi paste | 50 ml (2 fl oz) fish stock from above | 2 teaspoons shoyu or tamari sauce | ½ tablespoon extra virgin olive oil

ONE Heat the stock in a saucepan until boiling. Add the scallops and cover the pan, then turn off the heat and let the scallops poach for 2–3 minutes, depending how thick they are. Transfer the scallops to a serving dish with a slotted spoon. **TWO** To make the dressing, combine the wasabi paste, stock, shoyu sauce and oil and drizzle over the scallops.

Serves 4 with 2 other main dishes

NUTRIENT ANALYSIS PER SERVING 423 kJ – 100 kcal – 16.5 g protein – 3.2 g carbohydrate – 0 g sugars – 2.5 g fat – 0.5 g saturates – 0 g fibre – 210 mg sodium

MONKFISH STIR-FRIED WITH CELERY

Monkfish has a firm texture and virtually no small bones, which makes it ideal for stir-frying or braising. The juices from the monkfish combine with the distinctive taste of celery to give this dish a unique flavour. Serve with Roast Pork *(see page 84)*, stir-fried vegetables and a tofu dish.

INGREDIENTS 1 tablespoon rapeseed or olive oil | 3 slices fresh root ginger | 500 g (1 lb) monkfish fillets, cut into 1 cm (½ inch) thick slices | 100 ml (3½ fl oz) hot Fish Stock *(see page 22)* | 1 teaspoon shoyu or tamari sauce | 1 tablespoon Chinese rice wine or dry sherry | 1 teaspoon freshly ground white pepper | ½ teaspoon sesame oil | 500 g (1 lb) tender celery hearts, cut into 2.5 cm (1 inch) x 1 cm (½ inch) pieces

CORNFLOUR PASTE 2 teaspoons cornflour mixed with 2 tablespoons water or stock

ONE Heat the oil in a nonstick sauté pan over a high heat. Add the ginger and stir-fry for a few seconds until fragrant. **TWO** Add the monkfish and stir-fry for 1 minute, then add the hot stock and bring to the boil. Add the shoyu sauce, rice wine, pepper and sesame oil and stir. **THREE** Add the celery and bring the mixture back to boil, then add the cornflour paste, stirring until the sauce has thickened and has turned translucent.

Serves 4 with 2 other main dishes

NUTRIENT ANALYSIS PER SERVING 552 kJ – 130 kcal – 18.4 g protein – 5.0 g carbohydrate – 1.2 g sugars – 3.9 g fat – 0.6 g saturates – 1.3 g fibre – 132 mg sodium

HEALTHY TIP Celery contains phenolic acids, which have been shown to have anti-cancer effects; they have the ability to block the action of hormones called prostaglandins, which promote the growth of tumours.

recipe illustrated on pages 156–157

BREAM FILLETS WITH ORIENTAL DRESSING

INGREDIENTS 1 tablespoon rapeseed or olive oil │ 4 x 175 g (6 oz) red or black bream fillets │ 4 garlic cloves, crushed │ juice of 1 lemon │ 1 tablespoon chopped Thai basil leaves, to garnish

DRESSING 1 tablespoon Lemon and Fish Sauce *(see page 23)* │ 3 tablespoons Fish Stock *(see page 22)*

ONE Heat the oil in a nonstick sauté pan over a high heat until piping hot. **TWO** Add the bream fillets skin-side down and fry for 2 minutes. Turn the fillets over and put the garlic between the pieces of fish. Fry for 1 more minute then add the lemon juice and cook until it has almost evaporated. Transfer the fish fillets to a serving plate. **THREE** To make the dressing, mix the lemon and fish sauce with the fish stock. Drizzle the dressing over the fish fillets and garnish with the Thai basil leaves.

Serves 4 with 2 other main dishes

NUTRIENT ANALYSIS PER SERVING 836 kJ – 199 kcal – 30.9 g protein – 1.3 g carbohydrate – 1.0 g sugars – 7.9g fat – 0.4 g saturates – 0 g fibre – 330 mg sodium

HEALTHY TIP Bream is a white fish that is low in fat and high in protein and vitamin B12. It is ideal for people who are watching their weight.

STEAMED TROUT WITH BLACK BEANS

INGREDIENTS 1 teaspoon fermented black beans | 2 slices fresh ginger, peeled and finely chopped | 2 garlic cloves, finely chopped | 2 spring onions, sliced | 1 teaspoon shoyu or tamari sauce | 1 teaspoon olive oil | 375 g (12 oz) trout fillets, cut into pieces | 1 tablespoon roughly chopped fresh coriander, to garnish

ONE Pour about 5 cm (2 inches) water into a wok, place a metal or wooden rack in the wok and bring the water to boil. **TWO** Meanwhile, rinse the black beans in water to get rid of the excess salt. Put them into a small bowl and mash lightly with a fork. Mix in the ginger, garlic, spring onions, shoyu sauce and olive oil. **THREE** Place the fish pieces in a heatproof serving dish and thoroughly stir in the black bean sauce mixture, to ensure that all the fish pieces are coated. **FOUR** Set the dish on the wok rack, cover the wok and steam over a high heat for 6–8 minutes or until the fish is cooked. Sprinkle with coriander leaves and serve immediately.

Serves 4 with 2 other main dishes

NUTRIENT ANALYSIS per serving 547 kJ – 130 kcal – 18.2 g protein – 2.1 g carbohydrate – 1.2 g sugars – 5.5 g fat – 1.1 g saturates – 0.3 g fibre – 271 mg sodium

HEALTHY TIP Trout is an oily fish, which is an excellent source of omega-3 fatty acids. Some scientific studies have shown that oily fish may help to relieve some of the symptoms of the skin condition psoriasis.

RED THAI CURRY WITH TOFU AND MIXED VEGETABLES

There are three types of Thai curry – red, green and yellow – each made with different coloured chillies. Traditional Thai curries are made with whole coconut milk, which is high in fat. This recipe uses a reduced-fat version, but the end result is still deliciously creamy. To continue the South-east Asian theme, begin your meal with **Fresh Spring Rolls** *(see page 36)* **or Prawn and Grapefruit Salad** *(see page 48)*.

INGREDIENTS 1 tablespoon rapeseed or olive oil | 2 tablespoons red curry paste | 1–2 fresh green chillies, deseeded and sliced | 200 ml (7 fl oz) canned light coconut milk | 250 ml (8 fl oz) Vegetable Stock *(see page 21)* | 1 large aubergine, diced | 12 baby sweetcorn | 100 g (3½ oz) mangetout | 100 g (3½ oz) carrots, sliced | 125 g (4 oz) fresh shiitake mushrooms, halved | 1 large green pepper, cored, deseeded and sliced | 150 g (5 oz) canned sliced bamboo shoots, drained | 1 tablespoon Thai fish sauce | 1 tablespoon clear honey | 2 kaffir lime leaves | 1 x 394 g (13¾ oz) packet silken firm tofu, cut into 5 cm (2 inch) cubes

TO SERVE large handful of torn Thai basil leaves | handful of toasted cashew nuts

ONE Heat the oil in a large saucepan and fry the red curry paste and chillies for 1 minute, then stir in 2 tablespoons coconut milk (from the thicker part, which is at the top of the can) and cook, stirring constantly, for 2 minutes. **TWO** Add the vegetable stock and bring to the boil. Toss in the aubergine, then bring the mixture back to the boil and simmer for about 5 minutes. Add the remaining vegetables and cook for another 5–10 minutes. Stir in the fish sauce, honey, lime leaves and the remaining coconut milk and simmer for another 5 minutes, stirring occasionally. Add the tofu cubes and mix well. **THREE** To serve, top with the torn Thai basil leaves and toasted cashew nuts. Jasmine or Sticky Rice *(see page 225)* go best with this curry to absorb all the wonderful aromatic sauce.

Serves 4 with 2 other main dishes

NUTRIENT ANALYSIS PER SERVING 862 kJ – 254 kcal – 13.3 g protein – 13.8 g carbohydrate – 11.0 g sugars – 16.3 g fat – 5.7 g saturates – 4.8 g fibre – 482 mg sodium

HEALTHY TIP Mushrooms are a good source of potassium, which is needed for maintaining fluid balance in the body. They are low in calories but not if they are fried in oil. In traditional Chinese medicine, shiitake mushrooms are believed to bring a long and healthy life.

recipe illustrated on pages 166–167

CHILLI KALE

Kale is often maligned for being woody and inedible. Take time to pick over the kale leaves and choose young leaves wherever you can. Don't forget to remove the woody stalks when you're preparing them for this dish. Serve with a hearty casserole such as Spiced Beef and Vegetable Stew *(see page 76).*

INGREDIENTS 1 tablespoon olive oil │ 1 garlic clove, crushed │ 1 large white onion, chopped │ 500 g (1 lb) curly kale, stalks removed and leaves chopped │ 2 teaspoons lime juice │ 1 red chilli, deseeded and chopped │ 1 teaspoon gomasio salt │ ½ teaspoon freshly ground black pepper

ONE Heat the oil in a pan, add the garlic and onion and sauté for about 10 minutes or until the onion is translucent. **TWO** Add the curly kale and stir-fry for about 5 minutes. **THREE** Stir in the lime juice and red chilli, season with gomasio salt and pepper to taste and serve immediately.

Serves 4 with 2 other main dishes

NUTRIENT ANALYSIS PER SERVING 414 kJ – 98 kcal – 9.1 g protein – 6.8 g carbohydrate – 5.4 g sugars – 4.1 g fat – 0.5 g saturates – 8.3 g fibre – 150 mg sodium

HEALTHY TIP Kale is a good source of calcium, which is needed for strong bones and teeth, as well as for the healthy functioning of our nerves and muscles.

SESAME BROCCOLI

In this recipe blanched broccoli is dressed with a wonderful sauce made of sesame seeds, sesame oil, garlic and shoyu or tamari sauce. For a complete vegetarian meal, try this dish with Lentils with Lemon Grass and Lime Leaves *(see page 180)* and steamed or Boiled Rice *(see page 224)*.

INGREDIENTS 500 g (1 lb) broccoli florets | 1 teaspoon sesame oil | 1 tablespoon shoyu or tamari sauce | 1 garlic clove, crushed | 1 tablespoon toasted sesame seeds

ONE Blanch the broccoli florets in a saucepan of boiling water for a couple of minutes, then drain and place on a serving dish. **TWO** Make a dressing with the sesame oil, shoyu sauce and crushed garlic and pour it over broccoli. **THREE** Just before serving, sprinkle with the sesame seeds.

Serves 4 with 2 other main dishes

NUTRIENT ANALYSIS PER SERVING 286 kJ – 69 kcal – 6.3 g protein – 2.7 g carbohydrate – 1.9 g sugars – 3.6 g fat – 0.6 g saturates – 3.6 g fibre – 136 mg sodium

HEALTHY TIP Broccoli is an excellent source of vitamin C and beta-carotene. It also contains useful amounts of folate, iron and potassium.

SPICY TEMPEH WITH VEGETABLES

This dish takes its inspiration from Indonesia where tempeh (fermented soya beans) is often used as a protein alternative to meat, fish and eggs. Serve this dish with boiled wholewheat or egg noodles and eat it like a thick laksa.

INGREDIENTS 1 tablespoon rapeseed or olive oil │ 2 fresh red chillies, sliced │ 2 lemon grass stalks, finely sliced │ 2 kaffir lime leaves │ 1 large garlic clove, crushed │ 2 slices fresh root ginger, peeled and chopped │ 1 tablespoon tamarind paste │ 2 tablespoons Vegetable Stock *(see page 21)* │ 2 teaspoons shoyu or tamari sauce │ 1 tablespoon clear honey │ 500 g (1 lb) tempeh, cut into strips │ 125 g (4 oz) baby sweetcorn │ 125 g (4 oz) asparagus, halved

ONE Heat the oil in a nonstick sauté pan or wok over a high heat until piping hot. Swirl it around the pan then add the chillies, lemon grass, lime leaves, garlic and ginger. Turn the heat down to medium and stir-fry the spices for about 2–3 minutes. **TWO** Add the tamarind, vegetable stock, shoyu sauce and honey and cook for about 2–3 minutes until the sauce is thick and glossy. **THREE** Add the tempeh, sweetcorn and asparagus and stir-fry for about 2 minutes to warm them through.

Serves 4 with 2 other main dishes

NUTRIENT ANALYSIS PER SERVING 1185 kJ – 282 kcal – 27.0 g protein – 18.1 g carbohydrate – 10.6 g sugars – 11.1 g fat – 0.4 g saturates – 6.6 g fibre – 111 mg sodium

HEALTHY TIP Tamarind trees produce sickle-shaped pods with a fruity pulp, which has a slightly sharp and sour flavour. Tamarind paste is a concentrated form of pulp that can be used to flavour soups, salads, curries, meat and fish dishes. It is rich in vitamin C and fibre. In folk medicine, tamarind is thought to act as a laxative and as an antiseptic.

recipe illustrated on pages 172–173

MA-PO TOFU

This dish comes from Szechuan. It is traditionally cooked with minced beef or pork; this is a vegetarian version, but it still has the robust flavours of the original. The tofu acts like a sponge, soaking up the spices, so this dish tastes even better the day after you've made it. The spicy sauce in this dish is best appreciated with plain rice.

INGREDIENTS 5–6 dried Chinese mushrooms | 1 tablespoon rapeseed or olive oil | 2 garlic cloves, crushed | 2 fresh red chillies, deseeded and sliced | 300 ml (½ pint) Vegetable Stock (*see page 21*) | ½ tablespoon hoisin sauce | ½ tablespoon yellow bean sauce | 1 tablespoon shoyu or tamari sauce | 1 x 394 g (12¾ oz) pack silken firm tofu, cubed | 3 spring onions, thinly sliced, to garnish

CORNFLOUR PASTE 2 teaspoons cornflour mixed with 2 tablespoons water

ONE Put the dried mushrooms in a heatproof bowl, cover with boiling water and put a plate over the top of the bowl to keep the steam in. Set aside for 20–30 minutes. Drain the mushrooms, remove the stalks, then squeeze the water out of the caps and chop them roughly. **TWO** Heat the oil in a nonstick pan or wok until piping hot, add the garlic and chillies and stir-fry for a few seconds over a medium high heat. **THREE** Add the stock, hoisin, yellow bean and shoyu sauces, stir well and simmer for a further few minutes. **FOUR** Gently mix in the tofu and cook for a few minutes to heat through. **FIVE** Add the cornflour paste to the sauce, stirring gently to thicken. **SIX** To serve, sprinkle with the spring onions.

Serves 4 with 2 other main dishes

NUTRIENT ANALYSIS PER SERVING 548 kJ – 132 kcal – 9.1 g protein – 7.9 g carbohydrate – 0.6 g sugars – 7.2 g fat – 0.9 g saturates – 0.2 g fibre – 197 mg sodium

HEALTHY TIP Tofu is made by grinding cooked soya beans with water. It is then strained and mixed with gypsum (calcium sulphate) to solidify it into a curd. It is, therefore, an excellent source of calcium, particularly for people from the Far East who drink little milk and don't eat dairy products regularly.

STIR-FRIED TOFU WITH ASSORTED VEGETABLES

This is another classic way of serving tofu. The tofu is often deep-fried first to give it extra crispness; this adds more fat and calories, but it does taste delicious. You can achieve a similar crunchiness by roasting the tofu cubes with a little olive oil then stir-frying them with the rest of the ingredients. Serve this dish with steamed rice and Sea-spiced Aubergines *(see page 196)*.

INGREDIENTS 1 tablespoon olive or rapeseed oil | 1 slice fresh root ginger, peeled and finely chopped | 1 garlic clove, crushed | 1 teaspoon mixed pepper flakes | 75 g (3 oz) shiitake mushrooms, halved | 1 red pepper, cored, deseeded and cut into strips | 500 g (1 lb) bok choi, halved lengthways | 200 g (7 oz) fresh baby sweetcorn | 2 tablespoons shoyu or tamari sauce | 2 teaspoons hot pepper sauce | a few drops of sesame oil | 1 x 394 g (13¾ oz) pack firm tofu, cut into 1 cm (½ inch) cubes

ONE Heat a nonstick sauté pan over a high heat, add the oil and swirl it around to coat the pan. **TWO** Add the ginger, garlic and mixed pepper flakes and stir-fry for a few seconds. **THREE** Toss in the mushrooms and red pepper and stir-fry for a couple of minutes, then add the bok choi and sweetcorn and cook for about 2–3 minutes more. Season with shoyu, pepper sauce and sesame oil. **FOUR** Add the tofu and mix gently until heated through.

Serves 4 with 2 other main dishes

NUTRIENT ANALYSIS PER SERVING 1059 kJ – 255 kcal – 24.9 g protein – 8.3 g carbohydrate – 6.0 g sugars – 13.7 g fat – 1.7 g saturates – 6.5 g fibre – 673 mg sodium

HEALTHY TIP Tofu is a valuable source of protein and makes a great alternative to meat in many dishes. It is low in saturated fat and contains vitamin E.

STIR-FRIED BOK CHOI WITH SHIITAKE MUSHROOMS

INGREDIENTS ½ tablespoon rapeseed or olive oil | 500 g (1 lb) bok choi, halved lengthways | 20 fresh shiitake mushrooms, halved | 1 teaspoon shoyu or tamari sauce | 1 tablespoon Chinese rice wine or dry sherry | 3 tablespoons Vegetable Stock (see page 21)

CORNFLOUR PASTE ½ tablespoon cornflour mixed with 1 tablespoon water

ONE Heat the rapeseed oil in a nonstick sauté pan over a high heat until it is piping hot, swirling it round to cover the base of the pan. **TWO** Add the bok choi, a handful at a time, stirring occasionally. Cover the pan and cook for about 2–3 minutes, until the bok choi leaves have wilted slightly. Remove to a serving plate. **THREE** Return the pan to the heat and add the shiitake mushrooms. Stir-fry over a high heat for 30 seconds. Add the shoyu sauce, rice wine and vegetable stock and stir to mix. Add the cornflour paste slowly, stirring constantly until the sauce has thickened. **FOUR** Pour the mushrooms and sauce over the bok choi and serve immediately.

Serves 4 with 2 other main dishes

NUTRIENT ANALYSIS PER SERVING 343 kJ – 83 kcal – 7.3 g protein – 7.3 g carbohydrate – 3.4 g sugars – 2.3 g fat – 0.3 g saturates – 4.8 g fibre – 439 mg sodium

LENTILS WITH LEMON GRASS AND LIME LEAVES

Lentil dishes are rare in traditional Chinese main courses; they are usually used as a stuffing ingredient in rice dumplings wrapped in lotus leaves. This creamy lentil dish is best served with Sticky Rice *(see page 225).*

INGREDIENTS ½ tablespoon rapeseed or olive oil │ ½ tablespoon sesame oil │ 4 shallots, finely sliced │ 2 garlic cloves, crushed │ 2 red chillies, sliced │ 475 g (15 oz) Puy or dried brown lentils or yellow mung dhal, washed and rinsed │ 750 ml–1 litre (1¼–1½ pints) Vegetable Stock *(see page 21)* │ 2 dried kaffir lime leaves │ 2 lemon grass stalks, cut into 2.5 cm (1 inch) pieces and slightly crushed, plus extra to garnish │ 1 teaspoon grated lemon rind │ 2 tablespoons shoyu or tamari sauce │ large handful of torn Thai basil leaves (optional)

ONE Heat the oils in a saucepan over a high heat until hot, add the shallots, garlic and chillies and sauté for a couple of minutes. **TWO** Add the lentils and vegetable stock and bring to the boil. **THREE** Stir in the lime leaves, lemon grass, lemon rind and shoyu sauce, then reduce the heat and simmer for about 25–30 minutes, stirring occasionally to prevent the lentils from sticking to the bottom of the pan. Depending on which type of lentils you use, you may need to add more stock so that they don't dry up. Stir in the torn basil leaves, if using, garnish with the lemon grass stalks and serve immediately.

Serves 4–6 with 2 other main dishes

NUTRIENT ANALYSIS PER SERVING 1627 kJ – 384 kcal – 32.8 g protein – 56.8 g carbohydrate – 2.7 g sugars – 4.4 g fat – 0.8 g saturates – 0.5 g fibre – 267 mg sodium

HEALTHY TIP Lentils are low in fat and are a source of protein and fibre. Unlike meat, fish, poultry and eggs, they don't contain the ideal amounts of essential amino acids needed for growth and development so should be served with other plant or wholegrain foods, such as rice or bread, to make a 'complete' protein.

recipe illustrated on pages 182–183

QUAILS' EGGS WITH TOFU IN A CREAMY PEANUT SAUCE

Quails' eggs make an interesting addition to this tofu dish. Some people don't eat tofu because they feel it's too bland, but that's not so in this dish where the tofu takes on a spicy flavour from the creamy peanut sauce. This dish goes well with Steamed Buns *(see page 223)* or boiled egg noodles.

INGREDIENTS 125 g (4 oz) small button mushrooms │ 125 g (4 oz) shiitake mushrooms, halved │ 100 g (3½ oz) canned bamboo shoots, drained │ 1 x 394 g (13¾ oz) pack firm tofu, cut into 2.5 cm (1 inch) cubes │ 8 quails' eggs, hard-boiled and halved │ 1 tablespoon chopped fresh coriander, to garnish

CREAMY PEANUT SAUCE 4 tablespoons reduced-fat peanut butter │ 4 tablespoons Vegetable Stock *(see page 21)* │ 50 g (2 oz) plain soya yogurt │ 3 tablespoons rice wine vinegar │ 1 tablespoon shoyu or tamari sauce │ 1 garlic clove, crushed │ 2 slices fresh root ginger, peeled and finely chopped │ 1 red chilli, deseeded and thinly sliced │ 2 tablespoons chopped fresh coriander

ONE Make the peanut sauce by blending all the ingredients in a food processor until smooth. **TWO** Pour the sauce into a saucepan and heat gently until simmering. Add the button and shiitake mushrooms and the bamboo shoots and cook gently for 2–3 minutes. Add the tofu cubes and stir gently to warm through. **THREE** Transfer the mixture to a large serving bowl, arrange the halved quails' eggs over the top and sprinkle with the chopped coriander to serve.

Serves 4 with 2 other main dishes

NUTRIENT ANALYSIS PER SERVING 645 kJ – 154 kcal – 12.9 g protein – 7.5 g carbohydrate – 2.6 g sugars – 8.0 g fat – 1.2 g saturates – 1.1 g fibre – 235 mg sodium

HEALTHY TIP Eggs are an excellent source of vitamin B12, an important component for healthy nerves. Many people are concerned about their high cholesterol content (cholesterol is found only in the egg yolk) and its effect on blood cholesterol levels and the risk of heart disease. Heart experts recommend eating no more than 2–3 eggs per week.

ROASTED TOFU WIT SZECHUAN RELISH

INGREDIENTS 1½ tablespoons olive oil │ 1 x 394 g (13¾ oz) packet of silken firm tofu, cut into 2.5 cm (1 inch) cubes

SZECHUAN RELISH 250 g (8 oz) fresh tomatoes, diced │ 100 g (3½ oz) cucumber, diced │ 1 red chilli, deseeded and sliced │ 2 tablespoons thinly sliced spring onions │ ½ garlic clove, crushed │ ½ teaspoon soft brown sugar │ 1 tablespoon lime juice │ 2 tablespoons chopped fresh coriander │ ½ teaspoon freshly ground black pepper

ONE Pour the olive oil into a large foil-lined roasting tin and spread it with a brush. Arrange the tofu cubes evenly over the oil. **TWO** Put the roasting tin on the top shelf of a preheated oven, 240°C (475°F), Gas Mark 9, and roast for about 15–20 minutes or until the tofu is crisp and golden brown. **THREE** Meanwhile, make the Szechuan relish. Combine all the ingredients in a bowl and mix well. Set aside. **FOUR** Put the roasted tofu cubes on a serving dish and spoon over the relish.

Serves 4

NUTRIENT ANALYSIS PER SERVING 536 kJ – 129 kcal – 9.0 g protein – 3.9 g carbohydrate – 3.4 g sugars – 8.7 g fat – 1.2 g saturates – 0.9 g fibre – 12 mg sodium

FU YUNG WITH VEGETABLES

Fu yung means 'pretty face' in Chinese; it is a sort of scrambled egg omelette. You can also add cooked meats or prawns or toasted nuts to the dish, but don't be greedy and add too much or there won't be enough egg to bind the other ingredients. This dish goes well with **Sweet and Sour Pork** *(see page 82)* **and Vegetable Fried Rice** *(see page 226)*.

INGREDIENTS 2 teaspoons rapeseed or olive oil | 1 spring onion, finely sliced | 50 g (2 oz) carrots, cut into 2.5 cm (1 inch) lengths | 125 g (4 oz) fresh beansprouts | 50 g (2 oz) Chinese flowering chives, cut into 2.5 cm (1 inch) lengths | pinch of coarse sea salt | ½ teaspoon freshly ground black pepper | 4 eggs, lightly beaten

ONE Heat the oil in a nonstick sauté pan over a high heat until piping hot, swirling the oil around the pan. **TWO** Add the spring onion and carrots and stir-fry for a few seconds. Toss in the beansprouts, Chinese chives, salt and pepper and stir. **THREE** Pour in the eggs and scramble them with the vegetables over a medium to high heat. As the eggs start to set, fold the fu yung over in the middle to form a half-moon shape, move it back to the centre of the pan and continue cooking over a medium to high heat for 2 minutes. Toss or turn it over and cook the other side for 2 minutes. **FOUR** Serve immediately.

Serves 4 with 2 other dishes

NUTRIENT ANALYSIS PER SERVING 487 kJ – 117 kcal – 8.5 g protein – 2.5 g carbohydrate – 1.9 g sugars – 8.2 g fat – 2.1 g saturates – 1.0 g fibre – 85 mg sodium

HEALTHY TIP In the UK, some eggs are fortified with omega-3 fats, which are usually found only in oily fish. Eating these eggs can be helpful, particularly for people who don't like the taste of oily fish.

APPLE AND FENNEL SALAD WITH TOFU AND CHIVE DRESSING

It is rare to find salads on the menus of Chinese restaurants and takeaways. This recipe sets things right by combining the sweetness from the apples with the aniseed flavour of the fennel and rounding it off with a smooth tofu dressing. This salad goes well with Butternut Squash and Tofu Soup *(see page 55)*.

INGREDIENTS 2 sweet red apples, cored and sliced | 2 Chinese nashi pears, cored and sliced | 1 large fennel bulb, thinly sliced | 2 tablespoons toasted walnuts

TOFU AND CHIVE DRESSING 75 g (3 oz) silken tofu | 1 tablespoon rice vinegar | 1 tablespoon apple juice | ½ garlic clove, crushed | 2 tablespoons chopped fresh chives

ONE Blend all the ingredients for the dressing in a food processor. Pour into a screw-top jar and chill in the refrigerator until ready to use (it will keep for about a week in the refrigerator).

TWO Put the apples, pears and fennel in a salad bowl, add the dressing and toss until mixed. Sprinkle with the walnuts just before serving.

Serves 4 as a light meal

NUTRIENT ANALYSIS PER SERVING 1492 kJ – 359 kcal – 9.8 g protein – 30.1 g carbohydrate – 28.2 g sugars – 22.7 g fat – 1.9 g saturates – 7.3 g fibre – 24 mg sodium

HEALTHY TIP Sweet red apples are a good source of vitamin C, which helps to maintain a healthy immune system. In traditional Chinese medicine, apples are recommended to treat constipation.

recipe illustrated on pages 192–193

VEGETABLE CHOP SUEY

Fresh beansprouts are the main ingredient in a chop suey dish. You can add whatever combination of vegetables you like, as long as you don't overcook them. A little of whatever you fancy works brilliantly when making chop suey. The crunchy texture of the different vegetables goes really well with Spare Ribs *(see page 86)*.

INGREDIENTS ½ tablespoon rapeseed or olive oil | 1 teaspoon sesame oil | 1 large shallot, finely sliced | 1 garlic clove, chopped | 125 g (4 oz) fresh shiitake mushrooms, halved | 50 g (2 oz) canned water chestnuts, drained | 50 g (2 oz) canned bamboo shoots, drained | 350 g (11½ oz) fresh beansprouts | 2 spring onions, cut into 1.5 cm (¾ inch) lengths | 2 teaspoons shoyu or tamari sauce | ½ teaspoon freshly ground black pepper

ONE Heat the rapeseed and sesame oils in a nonstick sauté pan over a high heat until hot. Add the shallot and garlic and sauté over a medium heat for 1 minute until fragrant. **TWO** Turn up the heat to high, add the mushrooms, water chestnuts and bamboo shoots and stir-fry for 1 minute. **THREE** Quickly add the beansprouts, spring onions, shoyu sauce and pepper and stir-fry for about 30 seconds. Serve immediately.

Serves 4 with 2 other main dishes

NUTRIENT ANALYSIS PER SERVING 242 kJ – 58 cal – 3.6 g protein – 4.9 g carbohydrate – 2.6 g sugars – 2.8 g fat – 0.4 g saturates – 1.6 g fibre – 114 mg sodium

HEALTHY TIP Shallots belong to the same family as garlic. In scientific studies, plants from the allium family have been shown to increase the levels of good cholesterol in the body. This good cholesterol helps to carry the bad cholesterol away from the arteries in our bodies and so may help reduce the risk of heart disease.

SEA-SPICED AUBERGINES

This dish comes from Szechuan and is sometimes referred to as fish fragrant aubergine because the combination of spices is usually used to cook fish dishes. This version is less spicy than the traditional recipe but equally delicious. Discard the chilli seeds if you prefer a more mildly flavoured dish.

INGREDIENTS 750 g (1½ lb) aubergines │ ½ tablespoon olive oil │ 4–5 garlic cloves, finely chopped │ 2 slices fresh root ginger, peeled and finely chopped │ 1 red chilli, sliced │ 50 ml (2 fl oz) Vegetable Stock *(see page 21)* │ ¾ tablespoon yellow bean sauce │ 1 tablespoon Chinese rice wine or dry sherry │ 1 teaspoon shoyu or tamari sauce │ 2 spring onions, chopped, to serve

CORNFLOUR PASTE 1 teaspoon cornflour mixed with 1 tablespoon water

ONE Put the whole aubergines in a foil-lined roasting tin and bake in the centre of a preheated oven, 200°C (400°F), Gas Mark 6, for 30–35 minutes until they are soft and wrinkly. Remove and set aside to cool, then cut them into 2.5 cm (1 inch) cubes. **TWO** Heat the oil in a nonstick sauté pan over a high heat until hot, add the garlic, ginger and chilli and stir-fry for a few seconds until fragrant. Stir in the stock, yellow bean sauce, rice wine and shoyu sauce and bring to the boil. **THREE** Add the aubergine cubes to the sauce and simmer for about 5 minutes. **FOUR** Slowly stir in the cornflour paste and cook until the sauce has thickened and turned transparent. **FIVE** Sprinkle with spring onions and serve immediately.

Serves 4 with 2 other main dishes

NUTRIENT ANALYSIS PER SERVING 275 kJ – 65 kcal – 2.5 g protein – 8.1 g carbohydrate – 4.7 g sugars – 2.4 g fat – 0.4 g saturates – 4.2 g fibre – 124 mg sodium

HEALTHY TIP Aubergines can absorb large amounts of oil during cooking. If a recipe calls for aubergine slices, soaking them beforehand in salted water draws out the bitter juices and makes the flesh more dense and less likely to absorb large quantities of fat.

recipe illustrated on pages 198–199

RICE, LENTILS AND CHINESE MUSHROOMS

This mixture of ingredients is often used with fatty pork for the banana leaf dumplings, which are served during the Dragon Boat Festival on the fifth day of the fifth month in the Chinese lunar calendar. This recipe omits the fatty pork and is cooked in a saucepan, so it is less laborious and time-consuming but equally delicious.

INGREDIENTS 4–5 dried Chinese mushrooms │ 50 g (2 oz) mung dhal │ 250 g (8 oz) Thai jasmine rice │ 1 tablespoon rapeseed or olive oil │ 2 shallots, chopped │ 325 ml (11 fl oz) Chicken or Vegetable Stock *(see pages 18–21)* │ 5–6 fresh or frozen chestnuts, peeled │ 1 tablespoon chopped fresh coriander, to garnish (optional)

ONE Put the dried mushrooms in a heatproof bowl, cover with boiling water and put a plate on top to keep the steam in. Set aside for 20–30 minutes. Drain the mushrooms, remove the stalks, then squeeze the water out of the caps and cut them in half. **TWO** Wash the mung dhal in several changes of water, then soak for about 10 minutes to soften. Strain and set aside. **THREE** Rinse the rice thoroughly in a sieve and leave to drain. **FOUR** Heat the oil in a saucepan over a medium heat until hot, add the shallots, cover and sweat for 3–4 minutes over a low heat. **FIVE** Pour in the mung dhal and stir-fry with the shallots for a couple of minutes over a low heat. **SIX** Add the rice and stir to mix. Turn up the heat and pour in the stock. Bring the mixture to the boil, then reduce the heat to its lowest setting. Put the mushrooms and chestnuts on the top of the mixture, cover and simmer for 15 minutes. **SEVEN** Turn off the heat but leave the rice mixture on the hob for at least 20 minutes. Serve sprinkled with coriander leaves, if you like.

Serves 4 as a light meal

NUTRIENT ANALYSIS PER SERVING 1383 kJ – 326 kcal – 8.6 g protein – 4.5 g carbohydrate – 1.5 g sugars – 5.6 g fat – 1.1 g saturates – 1.1 g fibre – 7 mg sodium

HEALTHY TIP Unlike other nuts, chestnuts are high in starchy carbohydrates and fibre but low in fat. They are a good source of vitamin B6, which is needed for the proper functioning of the nervous and immune systems.

recipe illustrated on pages 202–203

BAMBOO SHOOTS, STRAW MUSHROOMS AND BROCCOLI

Fresh bamboo shoots are often very hard to find outside China, so this recipe makes use of the canned variety. Use bamboo shoot chunks if you can, as they are much crunchier and have a better flavour than the sliced versions. To make a complete vegetarian meal, serve this dish with Quails' Eggs with Tofu in a Creamy Peanut Sauce *(see page 184)*.

INGREDIENTS 1 tablespoon rapeseed or olive oil │ 2 slices fresh root ginger │ 1 garlic clove, crushed │ 1 tablespoon yellow bean sauce │ 500 g (1 lb) canned bamboo shoot chunks, drained │ 125 g (4 oz) canned straw mushrooms │ 100 ml (3½ fl oz) Vegetable Stock *(see page 21)* │ 2 tablespoons Chinese rice wine or dry sherry │ 250 g (8 oz) broccoli florets

ONE Heat the oil in a nonstick sauté pan or wok over a high heat until piping hot, add the ginger and garlic and stir-fry for a few seconds. **TWO** Add the yellow bean sauce and stir-fry for 1 more minute. **THREE** Toss in the bamboo shoots and straw mushrooms, stir and add the stock and rice wine. Braise for about 5 minutes over a medium heat. **FOUR** Turn up the heat, add the broccoli florets and stir-fry for about 3–4 minutes or until most of the stock has evaporated. Serve immediately.

Serves 4 with 2 other main dishes

NUTRIENT ANALYSIS PER SERVING 315 kJ – 76 kcal – 5.4 g protein – 3.2 g carbohydrate – 2.5 g sugars – 3.7 g fat – 0.7 g saturates – 3.9 g fibre – 170 mg sodium

HEALTHY TIP If you eat this as one of your main dishes, you can notch up two servings of vegetables in one sitting. You will also benefit from an increased intake of fibre, which helps maintain a healthy gut.

RICE AND N

OODLES

STIR-FRIED NOODLES WITH PEANUTS AND SWEETCORN

This recipe takes its inspiration from South-east Asia, where rice noodles are often eaten as snacks or light lunches rather than as part of a main meal.

INGREDIENTS 125 g (4 oz) dried thin rice noodles │ 2 tablespoons rapeseed or olive oil │ 2 garlic cloves, crushed │ 2 slices fresh root ginger, peeled and chopped │ 1 heaped tablespoon medium curry paste │ 250 g (8 oz) baby sweetcorn │ 250 g (8 oz) pointed cabbage, finely sliced │ 1 small red pepper, cored, deseeded and finely sliced │ ½ tablespoon Thai fish sauce │ 2 teaspoons shoyu or tamari sauce │ 60 ml (2½ oz) light coconut milk │ 100 g (3½ oz) roasted, unsalted peanuts, roughly chopped │ 2 tablespoons chopped fresh coriander │ 4 spring onions, finely sliced │ 2 tablespoons lime juice │ coriander sprigs, to garnish

ONE Put the rice noodles into a bowl of boiling water, cover and leave to stand for 5 minutes for them to soften. Drain and set aside. **TWO** Heat the oil in a large nonstick sauté pan over a high heat until piping hot. Add the garlic, ginger and curry paste and stir-fry for 2–3 minutes until the spices become fragrant. **THREE** Add the sweetcorn, cabbage and red pepper and stir-fry for about 5 minutes or until the cabbage has started to soften and wilt. **FOUR** Add the fish sauce, shoyu sauce and coconut milk. Stir to mix, then toss in the rice noodles and stir-fry until the noodles have warmed through. Turn off the heat and gently stir in the peanuts, coriander leaves, spring onions and lime juice. Garnish with coriander sprigs.

Serves 4

NUTRIENT ANALYSIS PER SERVING 2272 kJ – 557 kcal – 18.7 g protein – 72.0 g carbohydrate – 10.7 g sugars – 22.8 g fat – 4.5 g saturates – 7.0 g fibre – 464 mg sodium

HEALTHY TIP Sweetcorn contains two important plant chemicals, zeaxanthin and lutein. Scientific studies have shown that both of these act as antioxidants, which fight against damaging free radicals, particularly in the eyes.

recipe illustrated on pages 212–213

CHICKEN CHOW MEIN

Chow mein literally means fried noodles. In this dish the crispy, browned noodles soak up the sauce from the chicken and beansprout topping. If you like, you can spice it up with chilli sauce.

INGREDIENTS 200 g (7 oz) chicken breast, cut into thin strips | 225 g (7½ oz) wholewheat or egg noodles | 1 tablespoon rapeseed or olive oil | 2 garlic cloves, sliced | 2 teaspoons shoyu or tamari sauce | 300 ml (½ pint) hot Chicken Stock *(see page 18)* | 250 g (8 oz) fresh beansprouts | 2 spring onions, sliced

MARINADE ½ teaspoon cornflour | ½ teaspoon sesame oil | freshly ground white pepper

CORNFLOUR PASTE 2 teaspoons cornflour mixed with 2 tablespoons water

ONE Mix together the marinade ingredients and rub the mixture into the chicken strips. Set aside. **TWO** Put the noodles into a large bowl of boiling water, cover and leave to stand for 5–8 minutes or until they are soft. Drain and set aside. **THREE** Heat ½ tablespoon of the oil in a nonstick sauté pan over a high heat, add the garlic and stir-fry for a few seconds until slightly browned. **FOUR** Add the noodles with 1 teaspoon of the shoyu sauce and fry until crispy. Transfer to a serving plate. **FIVE** Heat the remaining oil in the same pan, add the chicken strips and stir-fry until they are almost cooked, then add the hot stock and the remaining shoyu sauce and cook for 1 minute. **SIX** Toss in the beansprouts and spring onions and stir-fry for 1 more minute. **SEVEN** Slowly add the cornflour paste and stir to thicken the sauce. Cook until the sauce has turned transparent then pour it over the crispy noodles.

Serves 4 as a light snack

NUTRIENT ANALYSIS PER SERVING 1445 kJ – 342 kcal – 21.0 g protein – 45.7 g carbohydrate – 2.6 g sugars – 9.7 g fat – 2.1 g saturates – 2.7 g fibre – 220 mg sodium

HEALTHY TIP Garlic is used a lot in oriental cuisine. Its health benefits have been touted for hundreds of years, yet it's only recently that some of these benefits have undergone scientific scrutiny. For example, research has shown that garlic has a beneficial effect on the way our blood clots, which has important implications for maintaining heart health.

HERBY RICE NOODLE SOUP WITH CASHEW NUTS

INGREDIENTS 225 g (7½ oz) dried medium rice noodles (ho fun) | 1.8 litres (3 pints) Vegetable Stock *(see page 21)* | 1 tablespoon shoyu or tamari sauce | 2 spring onions, sliced diagonally | 2 tablespoons chopped fresh coriander | 2 tablespoons chopped fresh mint | 125 g (4 oz) fresh beansprouts | 40 g (1½ oz) roasted, unsalted cashew nuts | ½ teaspoon sesame oil | 1 lime, cut into wedges

ONE Bring a large saucepan of water to the boil. Add the rice noodles, turn off the heat and cover the pan. Leave to steam for about 3–4 minutes, then drain. **TWO** Meanwhile, bring the vegetable stock to the boil. Add the shoyu sauce, reduce the heat and leave to simmer until ready to use. **THREE** Divide the rice noodles among 4 large bowls and top with spring onions, coriander, mint, beansprouts and cashew nuts. **FOUR** Divide the hot stock among the 4 bowls and serve immediately with the lime wedges.

Serves 4 as a light snack

NUTRIENT ANALYSIS PER SERVING 1255 kJ – 301 kcal – 6.2 g protein – 54.7 g carbohydrate – 1.4 g sugars – 5.5 g fat – 1.0 g saturates – 0.9 g fibre – 137 mg sodium

HEALTHY TIP Like all citrus fruit, limes are an excellent source of vitamin C. Lime juice makes a good alternative to salt.

NOODLES WITH AROMATIC PRAWNS

Rice noodles are very versatile and can be fried, served in soup or used to soak up the flavours from aromatic spices and prawns, as in this dish. They make a good alternative to boiled rice with a main meal.

INGREDIENTS 400 g (13 oz) raw prawns, patted dry with kitchen towel | 2 tablespoons olive oil | 400 g (13 oz) dried thin rice noodles | 4 garlic cloves, chopped | 3 red chillies, deseeded and chopped | 2 lemon grass stalks, finely chopped | 2 onions, shredded lengthways | 6 celery stalks, shredded lengthways | 4 teaspoons shoyu or tamari sauce | 3 spring onions, shredded lengthways | 3 tablespoons Lemon and Fish Sauce *(see page 23)* | freshly ground black pepper | 4 tablespoons crushed roasted unsalted peanuts, to serve | 2 red chillies, split lengthways, to garnish

ONE Mix the prawns with 1 tablespoon of the olive oil a small bowl and set aside. **TWO** Soak the rice noodles in hot water to cover. Leave for about 5–10 minutes until soft. Drain well, transfer to a serving plate and keep warm. **THREE** Heat a nonstick pan until very hot, add the prawns and sear on each side for about 30 seconds until golden brown. Remove from the pan and set aside. **FOUR** Heat the remaining oil, swirling it around to coat the pan. Add the garlic, chillies and lemon grass and stir-fry for about 30 seconds until the garlic is lightly browned. Toss in the onions and celery and stir-fry for a couple of minutes, until they have softened a little. **FIVE** Return the prawns to the pan, add the shoyu sauce and spring onions and season with pepper. Arrange on top of the noodles and drizzle with the Lemon and Fish Sauce. **SIX** To serve, sprinkle with the crushed peanuts and garnish with the red chillies. Serve the remaining sauce in a jug.

Serves 4 as a light main meal

NUTRIENT ANALYSIS PER SERVING 2599 kJ – 622 kcal – 28.4 g protein – 93.1 g carbohydrate – 7.3 g sugars – 14.0 g fat – 2.2 g saturates – 2.8 g fibre – 793 mg sodium

HEALTHY TIP Celery contains a plant chemical called apigenin, which has anti-inflammatory properties, so it may help to alleviate the painful symptoms of gout. It is also a good source of soluble fibre, which may help to lower blood cholesterol.

recipe illustrated on pages 220–221

STEAMED BUNS

INGREDIENTS ½ teaspoon dried yeast | 1 teaspoon sugar | 175 ml (6 fl oz) warm water | 275 g (9 oz) plain flour | 1 tablespoon olive oil | 20 small squares of greaseproof paper

ONE Put the dried yeast and sugar in a bowl, add the warm water, stir and leave in a warm place until the yeast becomes frothy. **TWO** Sift the flour into a large mixing bowl, add the yeast mixture and the oil and stir to mix. **THREE** Using your hands, work the mixture into a dough; you may need to add extra flour if the dough is too sticky to work with. Transfer it to a lightly floured surface and knead for about 5 minutes until the dough is smooth. **FOUR** Return the dough to the bowl, cover with a damp tea towel and leave to rise in a warm place for about 1½ hours or until the dough has doubled in size. **FIVE** Lightly knock back the dough for a few seconds then divide it into 20 pieces. Roll them into whatever shape you fancy – balls, knots, crescents – and put each one on a square of greaseproof paper to prevent them from sticking. Leave for 15 minutes to rise again. **SIX** Meanwhile, fill a wok two-thirds full of water, set a wok rack in the middle and bring the water to boil. Steam the buns in a large bamboo steamer, on high heat for about 10–12 minutes. Remove from the heat and serve immediately.

Makes 20 buns

NUTRIENT ANALYSIS PER BUN 226 kJ – 53 kcal – 1.4 g protein – 11.0 g carbohydrate – 0.5 g sugars – 0.7 g fat – 0.1 g saturates – 0.4 g fibre – trace sodium

HEALTHY TIP By replacing a quarter of the amount of plain flour with wholemeal flour, you can double the fibre content of these buns. The plain buns can be frozen; to reheat, steam them for 10 minutes over a high heat.

BOILED RICE

Many people think that boiled rice is bland, but that is not so in this recipe, where stock is used instead of water to enhance the taste. Remember that rice should not be cooked like pasta. Under no circumstances should it be rinsed under cold water after cooking to separate the grains of rice.

INGREDIENTS 350 g (11½ oz) Thai jasmine or long grain rice | 300 ml (½ pint) Chicken or Vegetable Stock *(see pages 18–21)*

ONE Put the rice in a sieve and wash it under running warm water, rubbing the grains together between your hands. This gets rid of any excess starch. **TWO** Put the rice into a saucepan and add the stock. Place the pan on the smallest ring on the hob and bring it to the boil. Give it a quick stir then reduce the heat to a simmer. Cover with a lid and leave to cook for 15 minutes. Turn off the heat and allow the rice to steam with the lid on for another 20 minutes. Don't be tempted to lift the lid to check what's going on. **THREE** To serve, fluff up the grains of rice with a spoon or fork.

Serves 4 as an accompaniment to a main meal

NUTRIENT ANALYSIS PER SERVING 1314 kJ – 314 kcal – 6.5 g protein – 70.0 g carbohydrate – 0 g sugars – 0.4 g fat – 0 g saturates – 0 g fibre – 0 mg sodium

STICKY RICE

INGREDIENTS 300 g (10 oz) glutinous rice | 750 ml (1¼ pints) water

ONE Wash the rice in several changes of water and drain. Put it in a large mixing bowl, cover with plenty of cold water and leave to soak for about 5–6 hours or overnight. **TWO** Drain the rice and wash it again, then drain thoroughly. **THREE** Heat some water in the bottom of a double boiler. Place the rice in the top pan and pour in enough water to reach about 1 cm (½ inch) above the rice. Cover and steam on a low heat for about 20–30 minutes. Remember to check the level of water in the bottom of the double boiler to prevent burning. If you don't have a double boiler, you can improvise by putting the soaked glutinous rice in a metal vegetable steamer and placing this over a saucepan of boiling water. Cover and steam for about 1 hour. You will need to check the water levels periodically to check that the saucepan hasn't boiled dry.

Serves 4 as an accompaniment to a main meal

NUTRIENT ANALYSIS PER SERVING 1127 kJ – 269 kcal – 6.3 g protein – 56.2 g carbohydrate – 0 g sugars – 1.2 g fat – 0 g saturates – 0 g fibre – 2 mg sodium

VEGETABLE FRIED RICE

This is a colourful and flavoursome way of using up leftover boiled rice. Special fried rice, which contains meat and prawns which increase the protein content, is often found on takeaway menus. This lighter version relies on crunchy vegetables. This dish goes well with **Roast Pork** *(see page 84)*.

INGREDIENTS 1 tablespoon olive oil │ 150 g (5 oz) carrots, diced │ 1 beaten egg │ 500 g (1 lb) hot boiled white rice cooked in Vegetable Stock *(see page 21)* │ 100 g (3½ oz) frozen peas, thawed │ 100 g (3½ oz) canned sweetcorn kernels, drained │ 100 g (3½ oz) canned pineapple chunks, drained │ 1 tablespoon shoyu or tamari sauce │ ½ teaspoon white pepper │ 2 tablespoons chopped spring onions, to serve

ONE Heat the oil in a nonstick wok or sauté pan and stir-fry the carrots for 1 minute, then add the beaten egg. **TWO** Add the cooked rice, peas, sweetcorn and pineapple and stir-fry for about 5 minutes. Season with shoyu sauce and white pepper. **THREE** To serve, mix in the chopped spring onions.

Serves 4 as an accompaniment to a main meal

NUTRIENT ANALYSIS PER SERVING 1572 kJ – 371 kcal – 9.4 g protein – 71.1 g carbohydrate – 9.0 g sugars – 7.5 g fat – 1.6 g saturates – 2.8 g fibre – 226 mg sodium

HEALTHY TIP Pineapple contains a good supply of vitamin C, fibre and potassium.

PRAWN FRIED RICE

This colourful fried rice recipe is my version of a very popular dish found on the menus of all Chinese restaurants and takeaways – special fried rice. This recipe doesn't include eggs or pork; instead it contains prawns and an assortment of vegetables.

INGREDIENTS 1 tablespoon rapeseed or olive oil │ 500 g (1 lb) fresh prawns, peeled and deveined │ 50 g (2 oz) shiitake or button mushrooms, halved │ 1 courgette, thinly sliced │ 1 small carrot, thinly sliced │ 50 g (2 oz) green beans, cut into 2.5 cm (1 inch) pieces │ 500 g (1 lb) hot Boiled Rice *(see page 224)* │ 2 teaspoons shoyu or tamari sauce │ 1 teaspoon freshly ground black pepper │ 1 spring onion, thinly sliced, to serve

ONE Heat the oil in a nonstick sauté pan until piping hot and stir-fry the prawns for 1 minute over a high heat. Remove the prawns and set aside. **TWO** Add the mushrooms, courgette, carrot and green beans and stir-fry for a couple of minutes over a high heat. **THREE** Stir in the hot rice and shoyu sauce, season with pepper and mix thoroughly. **FOUR** Return the prawns to the pan and stir-fry the rice mixture for a couple of minutes. **FIVE** To serve, sprinkle with the spring onion.

Serves 2 as a main meal or 4 with 2 other dishes

NUTRIENT ANALYSIS PER SERVING 2690 kJ – 636 kcal – 49.3 g protein – 90.5 g carbohydrate – 4.6 g sugars – 11.1 g fat – 2.0 g saturates – 2.6 g fibre – 609 mg sodium

HEALTHY TIP Shiitake mushrooms contain a special type of carbohydrate called lentinan. Trials have shown that extracts of lentinan can boost the immune system and thus increase our resistance to infections.

recipe illustrated on pages 230–231

RICE CONGEE

Rice congee or porridge is easy to make. It is often thought of as comfort food and has a huge fan base, ranging from young children to convalescents. This recipe uses leftover cooked rice. You can add whatever ingredients you fancy – some people like it with cooked chicken and spring onions or preserved duck eggs, while others prefer it plain and treat it more like a soothing soup to accompany a plate of noodles or dim sum.

INGREDIENTS 900 ml (1½ pints) Chicken or Vegetable Stock *(see pages 18–21)* | 225 g (7½ oz) cooked rice

ONE Bring the stock to the boil in a large heavy saucepan on the smallest ring on the hob. **TWO** Add the cooked rice, stir and partially cover the pan with the lid. Simmer for 30–45 minutes over the lowest heat, stirring occasionally to prevent the rice from sticking to the bottom of the pan.

Serves 4 as a light breakfast or snack

NUTRIENT ANALYSIS PER SERVING 294 kJ – 69 kcal – 1.2 g protein – 16.7 g carbohydrate – 0 g sugars – 0.2 g fat – 0 g saturates – 0.1 g fibre – 1 mg sodium

HEALTHY TIP Rice or faan is the staple food of southern China. It is a good source of carbohydrates and is gluten free. Because the bran is removed to make white rice, many of the vitamins and minerals are lost during the refining process, but you can now buy vitamin-enriched white rice. The healthiest alternative is, of course, brown or wholegrain rice, but often the Chinese will not treat this as a staple ingredient. If you gradually substitute small quantities of brown rice for white rice, you may come to prefer it.

DESSERTS

TAPIOCA PUDDING WITH COCONUT MILK

Tapioca is sometimes used in Chinese dessert soups. In this recipe, it is used to make a pudding, providing a background for the more intense flavours of mango and coconut milk.

INGREDIENTS 2 litres (3½ pints) water | 150 g (5 oz) pearl tapioca | 2 tablespoons elderflower cordial | 175 ml (6 fl oz) light coconut milk | 175 ml (6 fl oz) mango juice | 1 large mango, peeled, stoned and sliced

ONE Bring the water to the boil in a saucepan, add the tapioca and cook for about 20 minutes or until the tapioca is transparent. **TWO** Strain the cooked tapioca and divide it among 4 x 150 ml (¼ pint) jelly moulds. Chill in the refrigerator for about 2 hours until set. **THREE** Mix the elderflower cordial, coconut milk and mango juice in bowl. **FOUR** Unmould the tapioca puddings into individual bowls, spoon the coconut mixture over the top and serve the sliced mango on the side.

Serves 4

NUTRIENT ANALYSIS PER SERVING 739 kJ – 215 cal – 0.5 g protein – 46.1 g carbohydrate – 10.1 g sugars – 4.2g fat – 3.7 g saturates – 1.1 g fibre – 27 mg sodium

HEALTHY TIP Mango is a rich source of both beta-carotene, which can be converted into vitamin A by the body, and vitamin C. Both these vitamins act as antioxidants.

LYCHEE SLUSH

Lychees are Chinese fruit that are in season between November and January. They have a wonderful perfume and are best eaten fresh, but because of their short season this recipe uses canned ones.

INGREDIENTS 550 g (1 lb 2 oz) can lychees in natural juice │ 1 teaspoon finely grated fresh root ginger │ 1 teaspoon finely grated lemon grass stalk │ 75 ml (3 fl oz) water │ 125 ml (4 fl oz) lemon juice

ONE Drain the lychees and reserve the liquid. **TWO** Whizz the lychees, ginger and lemon grass in a food processor until smooth. **THREE** Combine the water, the reserved lychee liquid and the lemon juice in a saucepan over a medium heat. Add the puréed lychee mixture to the pan, stir to mix and heat to simmering point, then remove from heat and leave to cool. **FOUR** Pour the mixture into a freezer container, about 20 x 30 cm (8 x 12 inches), cover and freeze, stirring occasionally, until just firm, which will take about 1 hour.

Serves 4

NUTRIENT ANALYSIS PER SERVING 425 kJ – 599 kcal – 0.7 g protein – 25.7g carbohydrate – 25.6 g sugars – trace fat – 0 g saturates – 0.7 g fibre – 3 mg sodium

ALMOND JELLY WITH ASSORTED FRUITS

Soya milk is used in this Chinese dessert instead of the traditional evaporated milk, which makes it lower in fat and calories. As it is made with agar agar instead of gelatine it is suitable for vegetarians.

INGREDIENTS 1 litre (1¾ pints) water | 7 g (¼ oz) agar agar, cut up | 50 g (2 oz) caster sugar | 175 ml (6 fl oz) soya milk | 2 teaspoons almond essence | 250 g (8 oz) assorted fruits (e.g., mango, melon, kiwifruit and physalis), chopped

ONE Bring the water to the boil in a saucepan, then reduce the heat and add the agar agar. Allow it to dissolve slowly (it will take about 20 minutes), stirring occasionally. **TWO** Add the sugar and stir until dissolved. Remove the pan from the heat. **THREE** Stir in the soya milk, then strain the mixture through a fine sieve into a mixing bowl. **FOUR** Stir in the almond essence. Pour into 6 x 150 ml (¼ pint) jelly moulds and chill in the refrigerator for about an hour until set. **FIVE** To serve, unmould the jelly on to a serving dish and arrange the fruit around it.

Serves 6

NUTRIENT ANALYSIS PER SERVING 246 kJ – 58 kcal – 1.0 g protein – 13.0 g carbohydrate – 12.4 g sugars – 0. 6 g fat – 0.1 g saturates – 1.7 g fibre – 15 mg sodium

HEALTHY TIP Serving an assortment of fruits ensures that we top up on a variety of vitamins and minerals.

COCONUT PANCAKES WITH FRUIT

These light, fluffy pancakes are made with rice flour instead of wheat flour. The addition of reduced-fat coconut milk make these a firm family favourite, particularly if you enlist the help of kids in the preparation of the batter and allow them to stuff their own pancakes.

INGREDIENTS 150 ml (¼ pint) canned reduced-fat coconut milk | 100 g (3½ oz) rice flour | 150 ml (¼ pint) mango juice | 2 tablespoons rapeseed or olive oil, for frying | 300 g (10 oz) assorted fruits (e.g., papaya, pineapple, lychees or kiwifruit), chopped | 1 tablespoon toasted pumpkin seeds

ONE Make the pancake batter. Combine the coconut milk, rice flour and mango juice in a bowl. Beat well then leave the batter to stand for about 15 minutes. **TWO** Put ½ teaspoon oil in a small nonstick frying pan, about 15 cm (6 inches) across, and heat over a medium heat until piping hot, swirling the oil around the pan. **THREE** Spoon a thin layer of batter into the frying pan and cook until the top has set. Flip the pancake and cook the other side for about a minute. Remove the pancake and keep warm. Repeat until all the batter has been used, using ½ teaspoon oil for frying each pancake. **FOUR** To serve, put some of the fresh fruit in the middle of each pancake and roll it up. Scatter the pumpkin seeds over the top and serve immediately.

Makes 6 pancakes

NUTRIENT ANALYSIS PER PANCAKE 517 kJ – 147 kcal – 2.1 g protein – 21.7 g carbohydrate – 7.7 g sugars – 5.6 g fat – 2.6 g saturates – 1.4 g fibre – 17 mg sodium

HEALTHY TIP Pumpkin seeds make a nutritious addition to these pancakes. They are a useful source of iron, which is needed for healthy blood, and of zinc, which is required for growth and the development of a healthy immune system.

recipe illustrated on pages 244–245

TROPICAL FRUIT PLATTER

Traditionally, a Chinese meal ends with sliced oranges, which is a good way to include a portion of fruit as a matter of routine rather than effort. This recipe lists some fruit you might like to serve at the end of a meal on a hot summer day. I sometimes serve it with Lychee Slush *(see page 239)*, and sometimes I like to serve these fruits on banana leaves over a bed of ice.

INGREDIENTS 1 pineapple | 1 papaya | 2 kiwifruit | 2 star fruits (carambola) | 12 kumquats | 125 g (4 oz) strawberries | 125 g (4 oz) blackberries | fresh mint leaves, to decorate

ONE Chill all the fruits until cold. **TWO** When you are ready to serve, peel the pineapple, remove the core and cut it into large cubes. Peel the papaya, scoop out the seeds and slice lengthways. Peel the kiwifruit and cut into slices. Cut the star fruits into 2 cm (¾ inch) slices. **THREE** To serve, arrange the fruit on a large serving platter and scatter with mint leaves.

Serves 6

NUTRIENT ANALYSIS PER SERVING 264 kJ – 62 kcal – 1.1 g protein – 14.3 g carbohydrate – 0.4 g fat – trace saturates – 3.0 g fibre – 6 mg sodium

HEALTHY TIP Blackberries contain chemicals called anthocyanides, which act as anti-oxidants. Papaya contains vitamin C; half a papaya meets the daily adult vitamin C requirement. Kiwifruit is also an excellent source of potassium and vitamin C.

SESAME BANANAS

INGREDIENTS 500 ml (17 fl oz) apple juice │ ½ teaspoon ground cinnamon │ ½ teaspoon coconut extract │ 4 bananas, chopped into large chunks │ 125 g (4 oz) plain soya yogurt │ 1 tablespoon toasted sesame seeds

ONE Combine the apple juice, cinnamon and coconut extract in a saucepan. Bring the mixture to the boil, then reduce the heat and simmer for 5 minutes. **TWO** Add the bananas, cover and simmer for about 10 minutes or until the bananas are soft. Remove with a slotted spoon and divide among 4 bowls. **THREE** Stir the yogurt into the apple juice mixture to make a thick sauce. Spoon the sauce over the bananas and sprinkle with sesame seeds.

Serves 4

NUTRIENT ANALYSIS PER SERVING 775 kJ – 182 kcal – 2.5 g protein – 39.5 g carbohydrate – 36.9 g sugars – 2.7 g fat – 0.4 g saturates – 1.4 g fibre – 11 mg sodium

HEALTHY TIP Bananas are an excellent source of potassium, which is needed for the proper functioning of the nerves and muscles.

AVOCADO AND COCONUT SMOOTHIE

INGREDIENTS 250 ml (8 fl oz) calcium fortified soya milk │ 175 g (6 oz) soya yogurt │ 1 large ripe avocado, stoned and diced │ 2 tablespoons canned reduced-fat coconut milk

ONE Whizz the soya milk, yogurt and avocado in a blender until smooth. **TWO** Divide the smoothie between 2 tall glasses and top with a tablespoon of coconut milk. Serve immediately.

Serves 2

NUTRIENT ANALYSIS PER SERVING 1201 kJ – 303 kcal – 6.9 g protein – 14.7 g carbohydrate – 12.3 g sugars – 24.2 g fat – 5.9 g saturates – 3.5 g fibre – 94 mg sodium

HEALTHY TIP Avocados are a good source of vitamin E and potassium and also contain vitamins B1, B6 and C. Like olive oil, they are rich in monounsaturated fats, which are thought to help lower blood cholesterol levels. Avocados are a good source of fat, but even though they contain good fats they are high in calories.

RED BEAN SMOOTHIE

Red beans are an unusual ingredient in this smoothie recipe. This drink can be filling, so it makes a great afternoon snack if you're feeling peckish after a light lunch.

INGREDIENTS 1 litre (1¾ pints) water │ 125 g (4 oz) red aduki beans, soaked in water for 4 hours and drained │ 525 ml (17½ fl oz) calcium-fortified soya milk │ 3 tablespoons canned reduced-fat coconut milk │ crushed ice

ONE Bring the water to the boil in a saucepan, add the aduki beans and simmer over a low heat for 1–1½ hours until the beans are cooked. Remove from the heat and leave to cool. **TWO** Whizz the aduki beans and soya milk in a blender until smooth. **THREE** Divide the red bean mixture among 2–3 tall glasses and spoon some coconut milk over the top of each one. Add some crushed ice just before serving.

Serves 2–3

NUTRIENT ANALYSIS PER SERVING 601 kJ – 152 kcal – 10.3 g protein – 19.2 g carbohydrate – 3.4 g sugars – 4.3 g fat – 1.4 g saturates – 3.5 g fibre – 80 mg sodium

HEALTHY TIP Pulses such as aduki beans are low in fat as well as being good sources of protein and fibre. Pulses contain both soluble and insoluble fibre, which means that they can help to maintain a healthy gut as well as having the ability to help lower blood cholesterol levels.

INDEX

ACKNOWLEDGEMENTS

I would like to thank my family and friends who, over the years, have shared recipes, tips and many wonderful meals with me; in particular my father Wai Man Chan, husband Pak Sham and dear friends Dominic Lam and Brian Oliver. Thanks must also go to Brenda Wong and Eddie Chan at the Chinese Healthy Living Centre, Simon Lam and Thomas Chan at the Chinese Takeaway Association, and Sue Burke at William Levene. Finally, I am most grateful to Ken Hom, the author of my first-ever and favourite cookbook, for his encouragement and for writing the foreword.

The author and publisher would like to thank Blue Dragon for providing ingredients for the photography. For further information visit: www.bluedragon.com

EXECUTIVE EDITOR Nicky Hill

EDITOR Charlotte Macey

DEPUTY CREATIVE DIRECTOR AND DESIGN Geoff Fennell

SENIOR PRODUCTION CONTROLLER Martin Croshaw

PHOTOGRAPHY William Reavell/© Octopus Publishing

FOOD STYLIST Tonia George

PROPS STYLIST Liz Hippisley